"The doctrine of God's g[...]
And yet it has been misun[...]
Dr. Bing's book is a much-needed corrective to false concepts of
grace that are being taught today. Dr. Bing presents with remark-
able clarity the teachings of God's Word on grace for salvation
from sin and on grace for the Christian life. This book should be
read by every believer and every Christian leader."

—Roy B. Zuck, Th.D.

Senior Professor Emeritus of Bible Exposition,

Dallas Theological Seminary

Editor, *Bibliotheca Sacra*

"Some scholars complicate truth; others simplify truth. Dr. Bing
falls into the latter category. He has a unique ability to take com-
plex issues and boil them down to clear, straightforward principles
that are easy to understand. In *Simply by Grace* he untangles the
relationship between faith and works, grace and merit, effort and
trust. Thanks, Dr. Bing, for this excellent work."

—Dave Anderson, Ph.D.

President, Grace School of Theology

"There are some things in life that you cannot get too much of.
One of those is a biblical understanding of grace. The more you
grasp God's teaching about grace, the more it will grasp you. In so
doing, it will impact every area of your life. That's why Dr. Bing's
book is worth reading. Biblically based, easy to understand, and
thorough, it helps you see grace from God's perspective. Not only
is it instructional, his book will motivate you to live a life that testifies, 'By the grace of God I am what I am' (1 Cor. 15:10)."

—R. Larry Moyer, D.Min.

President and CEO, EvanTell

"The history of making sense of the universe finally got on track when the sun, not the earth, was understood to be the center of the solar system. Christianity, and your own spiritual journey, will get on track in the same way when grace, not law or works, is understood as the centerpiece of a life of faith. Dr. Bing has made the high truths of grace sit on the easy-to-reach shelf of practical living with this book. Plain, direct, and understandable; a grace resource for every library, small group, and home!"

—Fred Lybrand, D.Min.

Author, former pastor, and past president of
the Free Grace Alliance

"Dr. Bing portrays the clarity of the gospel with simplicity and grace. Where others pervert or attack the free gift of salvation, Dr. Bing effectively addresses their concerns with sound exposition of the Bible. When others misunderstand or misapply the high cost of discipleship, Dr. Bing provides a perspective that reflects the importance of living in godliness without confusing such efforts with the good news of salvation by faith alone. This book will be a welcome addition to the library of all who cherish the salvation provided *simply by grace*."

—Jack G. Lewis, Ph.D.

Associate Dean of Faculty, Moody Bible
Institute–Spokane

# SIMPLY *by* GRACE

## AN INTRODUCTION
## TO GOD'S LIFE-CHANGING GIFT

# CHARLES C. BING

Kregel
Publications

*Simply by Grace: An Introduction to God's Life-Changing Gift*

© 2009 by Charles C. Bing

Published by Kregel Publications, a division of Kregel, Inc., 2450 Oak Industrial Dr. NE, Grand Rapids, MI 49505.

**Library of Congress Cataloging-in-Publication Data**
Bing, Charles C., 1954-
  Simply by grace : an introduction to God's life-changing gift / Charles C. Bing.
    p. cm.
  Includes bibliographical references and index.
1. Grace (Theology) I. Title.
BT761.3.B56   2009   234—dc22   2009028829

ISBN  978-0-8254-2303-1

Printed in the United States of America

18  19  20  21  22  23  24 / 8  7  6

*To my wife,*
*Karen, who is*
*and has always*
*been God's*
*grace to me*

# CONTENTS

Foreword by Charles C. Ryrie . . . . . . . . . . . . . . . . . . . . . . 9

Introduction . . . . . . . . . . . . . . . . . . . . . . . . . . . . . . . . . 11

1. The Gift of Grace . . . . . . . . . . . . . . . . . . . . . . . . . . 15

2. The God of All Grace . . . . . . . . . . . . . . . . . . . . . . . 21

3. Surprised by Grace . . . . . . . . . . . . . . . . . . . . . . . . . 27

4. Saved by Grace . . . . . . . . . . . . . . . . . . . . . . . . . . . 37

5. A Maze of Grace . . . . . . . . . . . . . . . . . . . . . . . . . . 45

6. Secured by Grace . . . . . . . . . . . . . . . . . . . . . . . . . . 53

7. Assured by Grace . . . . . . . . . . . . . . . . . . . . . . . . . . 67

8. Grace and Good Works . . . . . . . . . . . . . . . . . . . . . 79

9. A New Accountability . . . . . . . . . . . . . . . . . . . . . . 95

10. A New Life . . . . . . . . . . . . . . . . . . . . . . . . . . . . . 107

11. A New Commitment . . . . . . . . . . . . . . . . . . . . . . 119

12. A New Freedom . . . . . . . . . . . . . . . . . . . . . . . . . 131

13. Sharing the Gift . . . . . . . . . . . . . . . . . . . . . . . . . 145

Notes . . . . . . . . . . . . . . . . . . . . . . . . . . . . . . . . . . . . 159

# FOREWORD

G
race distinguishes Christianity from all other religions, and grace can affect all areas and aspects of one's life. Yet grace, such a beautiful and important concept, is often misunderstood, limited in its applications, or mixed with impurities.

Dr. Bing makes none of these mistakes.

This book, which deals accurately and comprehensively with the subject of the grace of God, is needed and most welcome. Clear and easy to understand, it explores the many facets and ramifications of grace. Unequivocal in his positions, the author nevertheless represents other views fairly and kindly.

Today, errors regarding additions to and misstatements about grace abound in thinking, teaching, and preaching. Dr. Bing has dealt carefully with what the Bible says about grace in many areas. Salvation, justification, sanctification, security, assurance, and discipleship are examined accurately and clearly. Key Bible passages are plainly interpreted, and so-called problem passages are not avoided or strained to fit a preconceived conclusion.

To spend time in this book will not only sharpen and broaden one's understanding of grace, but will also deepen one's love and appreciation for the grace of God and the God of all grace.

CHARLES C. RYRIE, TH.D., PH.D.

# INTRODUCTION

A question posed years ago at a British conference on world religions sparked a lively debate: What makes Christianity unique among all the other religions in this world?

Some argued that it was the Incarnation, others, the Resurrection. But some replied that other religions had similar beliefs. When C. S. Lewis walked into the room, someone explained their quandary. "Oh, that's easy," he said. "It's grace."

How does Christianity distinguish itself from every other religion? *Simply by grace.*

How does a person become a Christian? *Simply by grace.*

How can a person be eternally saved? *Simply by grace.*

How can one know that one is eternally saved? *Simply by grace.*

How can one live the Christian life? *Simply by grace.*

How should a Christian be motivated to serve God and others? *Simply by grace.*

Do these seem like understatements or overstatements? They could seem like either unless you understand what God's grace is in its simplest meaning. Only when you understand the simplicity of His grace can you also begin to understand its deep riches.

*Simply by Grace* implies that the answer to a lot of confusion about salvation and the Christian life is found in a simple and accurate understanding of grace. I say this not to trivialize grace, but to rescue it from the encumbrances of those who confuse its meaning, complicate its simplicity, or teach it inconsistently.

*Grace* is a word commonly used among Christians and non-Christians, but too often it is misunderstood or at least under-appreciated. Christians, of course, believe in grace, or they really wouldn't be Christians because the Bible says, "By grace you have been saved" (Eph. 2:8). Non-Christian religions and quasi-Christian cults also use the word *grace* frequently. So what does it mean and why does it make a difference to us?

You might think that a consistent view of grace would result from intense Bible study, the kind someone would receive in a Bible college or seminary. But, having graduated with three degrees from such schools with three different groups of colleagues, and having interacted with many more people since then, I can tell you that there are vastly different views of grace. Churches differ in their views, pastors differ, professors differ, and therefore many Christians are confused.

In my study of the Bible and in teaching and preaching it for over thirty years, I've come to see that one's concept of God's grace is not only the key to becoming a Christian, but it is also the key to the assurance of salvation and living in freedom to serve God and others. That's why I've devoted my life and ministry to sharing the message of God's grace with people everywhere I go and however I can.

While it is my privilege to know many Christians who understand grace clearly, I've also met or read works by many others who have distorted God's grace to the detriment of those who need to be saved, those who are not sure they are saved, and those who need a firm foundation for Christian living. This distortion confuses the simple grace of God to the point of making it void. Between those who understand grace clearly and those who distort it is a larger group of people who use the language of grace and sing songs about grace, but have not applied its truth consistently or clearly in their beliefs about salvation and the Christian life.

Grace grounds us in the Christian life. If you don't understand the nature of grace, you will have problems and confusion in some area of life. You are not well-grounded in grace, for example, if

- you are confused about how to obtain eternal life.
- you are not sure that you ever had eternal life.
- you are not sure that you now have eternal life.
- you are not sure that you will keep eternal life.
- you have trouble feeling accepted by God.
- you don't feel like you have done enough to please God.
- you don't feel that you are good enough to please God.
- you are struggling with sin, guilt, and forgiveness.
- you have trouble forgiving others.
- you are judgmental toward others.
- you hate yourself.
- you hate others.

The list could go on, but getting grounded in God's grace will help resolve all of these issues and more. Those grounded in grace appreciate more fully what God has done in their salvation, and they are properly motivated to live a life that glorifies God. They accept more easily who they are, how God sees them, and how they should see others. They find a new power over their weaknesses and understand the gift of forgiveness.

This book is a discussion that introduces the major issues related to God's grace, helping you be well grounded in it. My prayer is that it will help you understand the beauty of the grace that gives us eternal and abundant life so that you can be free to be all that God made you to be—simply by grace!

# THE GIFT OF GRACE

A feast lay before me. One buffet was seafood, another Italian, and a third Mexican. Then there was, of course, the variety of salads and desserts. In the background a big band played rockin' big-band swing music, some of my favorites. It was a first-class wedding reception in an old plantation-style mansion at a picturesque country club in Louisiana. And I didn't know a single person there! Well, I knew the pastor friend who invited me to come along. He assured me the families would be glad to have me.

I was in town to speak at my friend's church, and he and his church folks were all attending the wedding and reception on this Saturday night, so rather than sit alone in someone's home, I went. I enjoyed a feast I didn't deserve. That would be a good illustration of what grace means.

But there's more to this story.

You see, the wedding was paid for well in advance by the bride's father, who knew he was dying of cancer. We watched a video tribute to him as we enjoyed his free gift to his daughter, her husband, and all their family and friends—and at least one stranger! I enjoyed a gift that I didn't deserve, which was paid for by someone I never knew. Now that is grace!

A feast awaits those who enter the truth about grace. Most know that the Bible speaks about grace and perhaps also know that grace has something to do with a gift. But that far from exhausts the depths of the beauty of grace or settles the confusion that surrounds the word. It shouldn't be this way, though. While grace is, indeed, a profound truth, it is a simple concept.

## THE MEANING OF *GRACE*

A little background will help you understand grace. The word *grace* is found in the English Bible about 148 times, depending on the version you read.[1] In the English translation of the Old Testament, *grace* is used about twenty times and translates a couple of different words from the original Hebrew. In the New Testament it is used 128 times and mostly translates one word from the Greek.

Just as does English, the Old Testament reflects some general uses of the word. In English people use the word *grace* to denote a prayer said before dinner, or to describe a thing of beauty or an elegant performance. In the Old Testament, *grace* sometimes translates the idea of beauty or charm, but the main Hebrew word that is translated *grace* comes from the word that means "to show favor." Some think that this Hebrew word comes from the idea of someone who is in a superior position bending or stooping to help a needy person who is in an inferior position. I like what a popular pastor once said: "Love that goes upward is worship. Love that goes outward is affection. Love that stoops is grace."[2] Grace is God's loving way of meeting our needs by showing us favor we do not deserve.

A story from the Old Testament book of Ruth helps us visualize what grace means. Three times in chapter 2, Ruth refers to finding favor with a man named Boaz (vv. 2, 10, 13). To appreciate what this means we must know that Ruth was a starving Gentile Moabite widow—a loser on four counts in the eyes of the Jews. She traveled to Israel with her mother-in-law, Naomi, to find food and help. Ruth goes to the fields to glean leftover heads of grain, hoping to find food and perhaps favor with Boaz, the very rich landowner. Boaz notices her and offers her his fields to glean, his protection, water, food, and eventually his hand in marriage. The rich Boaz stooped to help the lowly Ruth in her desperate need. But his grace was not just metered in meals, it was lavished in love.

The word *grace* can also be used in some general ways in the New Testament, for example, as a greeting or blessing.[3] But more importantly, in the New Testament *grace* is used as a specific word that defines theological truths about eternal salvation and the Christian life.

The New Testament book that best helps us understand grace is Romans. No wonder, because that book uses the word *grace* twenty-eight times—more than any other New Testament book. Romans explains how grace makes us acceptable to God and how it helps us live to please Him. Romans also supplies a couple of key descriptions of grace.

## AN UNCONDITIONAL, FREE GIFT

The word usually translated as "grace" in the New Testament is the Greek word *charis*. It simply means "a free gift." By free, we mean that it is totally undeserved; nothing that a person does, commits, surrenders, or promises can earn or merit grace. It is therefore an unconditional gift. By *unconditional* we mean that God, as the Giver of grace, does not put any such conditions on people before they can receive His gift. When someone tries to earn the gift of grace, it ceases to be grace. Romans 4:4 says, "Now to him who works, the wages are not counted as grace but as debt."

Grace, then, is a gift given freely and without conditions. If we work for it, it is no longer grace but a wage, a paycheck for our work. When it comes to our eternal salvation, God does not pay wages. He gives eternal life only as a gift. When you receive a paycheck for a week of hard work, do you tell your employer, "Thanks so much for this wonderful blessing—I really don't deserve it"? It's more likely that you feel you deserve to be paid more!

Another defining passage, Romans 11:6, says that the concepts of works and grace should not be confused: "And if by grace, then it is no longer of works; otherwise grace is no longer grace. But if it is of works, it is no longer grace; otherwise work is no longer work."

The concept of earning or meriting something based on who we are or how we perform is contrary to the biblical concept of free, unmerited, unconditional grace. The concepts of work and grace are mutually exclusive. They do not mix any more than do oil and water.

Suppose your neighbor washes your car as an act of kindness, not expecting or wanting anything from you in return. That would be an act of grace. Even if you were to reciprocate and give him something as a reward, and even if he took it, that would not compromise his pure act of grace. If, however, your neighbor *requires payment before* he will wash your car, grace is totally negated. Instead of giving you grace, he is now requiring a payment. Unconditional grace cannot be conditioned on any work, payment, or promise.

## A SPIRITUAL GIFT

Grace as a gift is sometimes expressed by the Greek word for spiritual gift, *charisma*, which comes from the same Greek word for grace as above, *charis*. God gives Christians spiritual gifts for use in ministry. They are not earned or achieved; they are bestowed by God, the Giver of all good things. These words for gift and grace are combined in 1 Peter 4:10: "As each one has received a gift [*charisma*], minister it to one another, as good stewards of the manifold grace [*charis*] of God."

Just as no one can earn or deserve God's specific spiritual gifts, neither can anyone earn or deserve God's gift of eternal life. Understanding that grace is God's free gift to us is the first step in becoming grounded in grace. By *gift*, we mean that it is absolutely free, unconditional, and undeserved. Any other definition of grace has serious repercussions for one's view of salvation, assurance of salvation, the Christian life, and ministry. Any attempt to be worthy of it, to deserve it, to merit it, to trade a commitment for it, or to perform at a certain level for it will negate grace so that it ceases to be grace.

Those who are not grounded in a clear understanding of God's absolutely free grace will not find peace and rest in their relationship with God and others. That may sound severe, but think about it: if grace must be earned or deserved, we could never know when we've done enough to earn it or when we're good enough to deserve it. Knowing that grace is absolutely free allows us to enjoy our relationship with God, ourselves, and others, and it gives God the infinite pleasure of giving us a gift, because, as we will see in the next chapter, He is "the God of all grace."

## REVIEW QUESTIONS

1. What is biblical grace?
2. Explain and expand the idea of "unconditional" in relation to grace.
3. Explain how grace and works are related.
4. Why is it so important to understand that grace is absolutely free?

# THE GOD OF ALL GRACE

We cannot understand grace until we understand where it comes from and how it has unfolded in God's purpose for the world. Grace is a persistent theme in biblical history. The grace we enjoy today is the same grace God has always offered to the world. To understand it fully, we must understand where it comes from or, rather, *who* it comes from. In short, it comes from God's infinite love for us.

The Bible describes the character of God in many ways. Perhaps the chief characteristic God shares with us is His love. "God is love," the Scriptures say (1 John 4:8). The primary way that God communicates His love is through His grace, which meets our every need. The apostle Peter called Him "the God of all grace" (1 Peter 5:10). It is a fundamental characteristic of God that, because He loves us so, He does not deal with us as we deserve, but gives us freely what we do not deserve. The gracious character of God is demonstrated in His treatment of mankind throughout history.

## A STORY OF GRACE

It was an act of grace to create human beings in the first place. God created and designed us to rule the earth (Gen. 1:26–28) as we enjoy life, which is another way of saying that He made us to enjoy Him because He is Life. But when the first man, Adam, listened to Satan and disobeyed God, he experienced death and brought death to us all as his descendants. Death must be understood not simply as the cessation of physical life, but as separation from God. Adam did not die physically the moment he disobeyed God by eating the forbidden fruit. He died spiritually because he became separated from God.[1]

The story of the Bible is the story of God restoring the original position and the life lost by mankind. When Adam and Eve sinned, they were naked and ashamed and hid from God. God was gracious to cover them with animal skins and hide their nakedness. Then God promised that He would send a Person, an Offspring of the woman, who would destroy Satan and his power of death (Gen. 3:15). The promise of a Deliverer was not conditioned on anyone deserving it. Rather, the promise was made for those who did not deserve it in any way. All that could be done was to believe God's promise and wait for it to be fulfilled.

God's grace got more specific when He chose one man, Abraham, to begin a special people who would become the instruments of His grace. God promised to Abraham a land, a special Descendant, and a blessing for the whole world. Why Abraham? No reason is given, but after the promise was made to him, Abraham was faithful and obedient, though not perfect. Still the promise is reiterated to him and to his son, Isaac, as well as to his grandson Jacob.[2] God's promise is guaranteed to all three generations with the words "I will give . . . ." God did not say "I will give *if* . . . " making the fulfillment of the promise something to be earned or deserved. Instead the fulfillment depended on God and His gracious character. It was a free gift to those who did not deserve it. Both Isaac and Jacob showed their imperfections in episodes of deceit,[3] but God's promise was not jeopardized; it depended on *His* faithfulness to His own word, not on the faithfulness of flawed human beings.

So, through Abraham, God began a special people of promise, the Jews. Why the Jews? Not because they deserved God's blessing. Their history is one of consistent and persistent disobedience. We would agree with the person who quipped, "How odd of God to choose the Jews!" We can only surmise that God chose the Jews simply because He sovereignly chose them.

God's grace persisted throughout biblical history. His promise became more specific to King David when He promised that a Descendant of David would sit on the throne of the kingdom forever. The Descendant first promised in Genesis is revealed to be a king like David and from David.[4] Why David? Again, not because he was worthy of God's grace. David's life was marred by some major sins. But God's grace is always undeserved and, therefore, its realization rests in God's faithfulness to His own character and word, not on human performance.

## JESUS FULL OF GRACE

The fulfillment of God's promised deliverance came in Jesus Christ, the Descendant of David, who will become the King of the Jews. Jesus was God Himself embodied in a human being miraculously born to a woman. God stepped out of eternity and into human history so that His promise would be fulfilled. Jesus was described as "full of grace and truth" (John 1:14), meaning that He was the ultimate expression of God's undeserved favor toward us, and the ultimate fulfillment of God's promise to us. Jesus came to earth not because we deserved Him. On the contrary, He came into a world dark with evil, a world that rejected Him. Even His own people, the Jews, rejected Him.[5]

When he walked the earth, people saw in Jesus the embodiment of God's grace. As He proclaimed the truth about the kingdom of God, He also taught about God's loving compassion. His actions displayed the balance of grace and truth as He rebuked those who opposed God's truth but healed and helped those with needs. Jesus' actions and attitudes were characterized by love, patience, kindness, and gentleness toward others. The grace and truth of Jesus Christ reached its climax when He voluntarily gave His life on the cross then rose from the dead to meet our need as sinners, all according to the Scriptures' expectation.

Jesus Christ conveys God's loving grace to a needy world of undeserving sinners. That is why the Bible says that in Jesus "the grace of God that brings salvation has appeared to all men" (Titus 2:11). The God-Man who embodied God's grace is our Deliverer from sin and death, who restores us to our relationship to God and His purpose for us. Jesus gives life to us sinners because He is life, God's life.

But why sinners? Consistent with the character of God throughout all His dealings with the world, Jesus does not give life to those who deserve it (because none do!). Instead, he gives life to those who *do not* deserve it, those who desperately need it.

## GRACE TODAY

When we talk about how God saves people from sin, there is no other explanation except *simply by grace*. The best of us is not perfect, and only perfection could earn God's life—which is eternal life—and the forgiveness of our sins. God does not trade His salvation for any commitment or promise we make because He knows our best commitment will eventually fall short. Salvation must depend on God—*His* character, *His* promise, *His* work, *His* commitment to us.

The history of mankind in the story of the Bible is one in which a loving God gives salvation as a free gift. It has always been that way and always will be. It is this way today and for you. Yes, it sounds too good to be true, but unless you believe this, you will never be grounded in grace and enjoy God's life.

Now you might be thinking, isn't God also a just God? Doesn't His justice demand that our sinfulness be punished? The answer to that lies in what Jesus Christ did to satisfy God's justice for us.

## REVIEW QUESTIONS

1. How would you relate God's love with His grace? His justice with His grace?

2. Explain how the history of the Jews testifies to God's grace.

3. Why is Jesus described as "full of grace and truth"?

4. What parallels do you see between God's gracious dealings throughout biblical history and your own eternal salvation?

# SURPRISED BY GRACE

G race is so difficult for some people to accept or understand because it is something they do not expect.

We *expect* God's justice—we know our sin deserves it.

We *hope* for God's mercy—that He would not give us what we deserve.

We are *surprised* by His grace—that He gives us blessings we do not deserve!

Some time ago I had lunch with a friend at a restaurant, and at the end of our time together I went to the restroom. When I left the restroom I absentmindedly went to my car without paying for my lunch. A half mile down the road I realized this and felt terrible, so I went back. When I walked into the restaurant, I expected justice—surely the staff had called the cops, or at least gotten very angry. I hoped for mercy—that they would accept my apology and let me pay them. But I was surprised by grace—they told me that my friend had secretly paid for my lunch before he left!

Two criminals hung on crosses beside Jesus. The first evidenced no guilt for his crimes. But the second showed that he *expected* the justice he deserved when He said, "We receive the due reward of our deeds." He *hoped* for mercy, or that Jesus would show favor toward him, when he said, "Lord, remember me when You come into Your kingdom." But he was *surprised* by grace when Jesus said, "Today you will be with Me in Paradise."[1]

We are conditioned to expect justice in our graceless world. Lawbreakers are punished. Good grades and wages must be earned. We expect to get what we deserve. When we get something better than we deserve, we look at it as too good to be true. If we are ever convinced that it is true, we are surprised!

## WHY WE NEED GOD'S GRACE

We need God's grace because we have all sinned and deserve the judgment that justice demands—separation from God now and in eternity. The Bible makes that very clear and unarguable: "For all have sinned and fall short of the glory of God" (Rom. 3:23).

Every person has failed to measure up to God's perfection. We all need to experience pardon from our penalty and be given God's eternal life. But our sin is so serious that we cannot pay for it by doing good or being good. "Therefore by the deeds of the law no flesh will be justified in His sight, for by the law is the knowledge of sin" (Rom. 3:20). In other words, doing deeds that the Old

Testament Law demands or keeping any other set of rules of conduct cannot make us acceptable to God.

To be justified means to be made acceptable to God judicially, to be declared righteous before God. As the supreme Judge, God has the power in His courtroom to declare anyone righteous in His sight. When the Bible says that God justifies someone, it does not mean that that person instantly becomes righteous in character and conduct. That person does, however, become instantly acceptable to God, that is, righteous in a legal sense. In other words, as a just Judge, God cancels the penalty for sin—which is death—and declares the sinner acceptable because that person now has Jesus Christ's "acceptability," or righteousness, imputed (credited) to him or her. The person who was dead in sin now has eternal life and begins a new relationship with God.

We need grace also because God's standard is too high and our best efforts are too low. His standard is His own perfect righteousness. That perfect righteousness was reflected in the Old Testament Law, the core of which is represented in the Ten Commandments:

- Do not have any gods other than the true God.
- Do not make false images of God.
- Do not take God's name in vain.
- Keep the Sabbath holy.
- Honor your parents.
- Do not murder.
- Do not commit adultery.

- Do not steal.
- Do not lie.
- Do not covet.

Everyone would probably admit to breaking at least one of the Ten Commandments (who hasn't told a lie?). But when we interpret them the way Jesus did, we see that we are even more guilty than we thought. We may have never physically murdered someone, for example, but Jesus said, "You have heard that it was said to those of old, 'You shall not murder, and whoever murders will be in danger of the judgment.' But I say to you that whoever is angry with his brother without a cause shall be in danger of the judgment" (Matt. 5:21–22).

By this standard, anyone who has never physically committed murder would certainly be guilty of mental murder—an unjust anger toward someone. Likewise, we may have never had an immoral sexual relationship, but Jesus interpreted adultery more broadly when he said, "You have heard that it was said to those of old, 'You shall not commit adultery.' But I say to you that whoever looks at a woman to lust for her has already committed adultery with her in his heart" (Matt 5:27–28). Again, according to Jesus, those who might be innocent of the outward sinful act are still guilty because of the inner sinful thought.

When we interpret God's standard of righteousness as not simply the physical act, but include the thought and motive, we would probably admit to breaking all ten of the commandments! His standard is unattainably high.

When we understand that God's standard is too high, we will see that our best efforts are too low. First, our debt is too great: "all have sinned." Sin is anything that falls short of God's perfection or breaks His commands. That crime demands justice. The just penalty for sin is death, or separation from God. But that payment cannot be made by good deeds. To think it can be paid by our works underestimates the perfect holiness (otherness) of God, as if His perfect infinite standard could be satisfied by our pitiful finite payments. Even that notion incurs more guilt, because it insults God's character.

Further, even our good deeds are tainted. That is why we read, "There is none who does good, no, not one" (Rom. 3:12). At first glance, this statement doesn't seem to reflect reality, because we see people, including non-Christians, doing good deeds—helping their neighbors, giving to charities, building hospitals, working for the humane treatment of animals, and so forth. But the truth is that a good deed done in the context of rebellion is not good in God's eyes. In other words, if someone rejects God's gift of His Son, anything meant to earn favor with God or promote one's self is nothing but an insult. Let's imagine that a mother sends her young son to his room and tells him to stay there until his room is clean. But without cleaning the room, he sneaks out the window and washes her car. Is that a good deed? Not if we understand that it was done in a context of disobedience and rebellion.

Further, our best efforts are not good enough because our idea of good isn't good enough. We often use *good* in a relative sense.

A man or woman is good only to the extent that he or she is better than most people we know. That person is not perfect, and someone is certainly better. But when we talk about good in relation to God, we are speaking of absolute or perfect goodness. The Bible tells about a young man who thought he was good and then called Jesus "Good Teacher." Jesus' answer is incisive: "Why do you call Me good? No one is good but One, that is, God" (Matt. 19:17).

While the young man conceived of goodness in a relative way—he was better than most people—Jesus spoke of good in an absolute way, with God as the ultimate measure of goodness. And so Jesus showed us the uncrossable distance between the two understandings of good. That is why Romans 3:12 says that no one is righteous. We may do good and righteous-looking things, but we are not as good or as righteous as God.

The only possible conclusion from our sinfulness is given to us in Romans 3:19–20:

> Now we know that whatever the law says, it says to those who are under the law, that every mouth may be stopped, and all the world may become guilty before God. Therefore by the deeds of the law no flesh will be justified in His sight, for by the law is the knowledge of sin.

So we are all guilty before God and cannot open our mouths with a reasonable defense. The Old Testament Law and God's moral principles inscribed on every human heart were never intended to help us earn God's righteousness. They were given to show us our sin. We can compare the law to an X-ray machine. We get an X-ray to see what the problem is inside of us, but we do not expect the X-ray to heal us of that problem. But when we know our problem, then we can seek the proper treatment.

To understand the progress of thought in Romans is to understand that when we come to Romans 3:20 we are rightfully and totally condemned as sinners before God. The apostle Paul has painted the darkest picture of our situation. We have a problem and can do nothing to save ourselves from God's justice. We cannot cure being bad by doing good. We need help from outside of ourselves!

## GOD'S ANSWER TO OUR PROBLEM

You must appreciate the next words in Romans 3:21—*But now* . . . With these pivotal words, the apostle Paul declares what God has done about our problem. We are not left in darkness or despair; we are not left to pay for our sins by eternal separation from God.

*But now . . .*

What a blessed contrast these words signify! We are not left under condemnation. God has solved our problem, but it wasn't through the Old Testament Law or our efforts to do and be good. "But now the righteousness of God apart from the law is revealed, being witnessed by the Law and the Prophets, even the righteousness of God, through faith in Jesus Christ, to all and on all who believe" (Rom. 3:21–22).

We can have God's righteousness credited to us through faith in Jesus Christ as the one who satisfied God's justice on our behalves. He then rose from the dead to offer us His eternal life. Faith is the means by which we receive that eternal life when we have Christ's righteousness credited to us. The judicial declaration that we are now considered righteous before God is called justification.

## A GIFT COSTS SOMEONE SOMETHING

How can God pardon the guilty and make them instantly acceptable to Himself while maintaining His character of justice? How can justification be free when God demands that sin be punished by death? Since we could not be declared righteous by our performance, God had to do what we could not. Consider this very important verse that follows the statement that we are all sinners: ". . . being justified freely by His grace through the redemption that is in Christ Jesus" (Rom. 3:24).

This verse tells us how we who are sinners can be justified. As explained earlier, to be justified means to be declared righteous or acceptable to God. In the eyes of the Law we are no longer viewed as Lawbreakers. In fact, God views us in the same way He views His own Son—perfectly righteous in our standing before Him.

Every word in verse 24 is important. Our justification is "freely by His grace." If you are observant, you might be wondering why the word *freely* is used, because grace already means a free gift. Isn't that being redundant? Yes, it is. But repetition in the Bible usually means that something is being emphasized. God is emphasizing the *absolute freeness* of His grace. We can never earn His grace by being good enough, or by doing enough good things, or by not doing bad things.

But how can our justification—that is, our eternal salvation—be given to us as a totally free gift? The same verse tells us that the gift is free to us because it has been paid for by another—Jesus Christ. The word *redemption* speaks of a price that has to be paid to set something free. That price was not paid by us; it was paid by Jesus Christ, God the Son. Only His sinless life could be an acceptable payment for the sins of each and every one of us so that we could be set free from sin's condemnation.

Jesus did not inherit our sinfulness because He was conceived by the Holy Spirit and born of a virgin. He then lived a perfect, sinless life. When He died on the cross, He was the perfect sacrifice that could pay the price for any sin no matter how serious. Not only was He a perfect sacrifice, but because He was God in the flesh, He was also an eternal sacrifice that could be applied to everyone, everywhere, anytime. When He rose from the dead, He showed himself to be not only the Giver of eternal life, but also Life itself.

Every gift costs the giver, not the recipient. The gift of grace cost somebody something. It cost God His only Son. That is how it can be totally free to us. We are saved by a life we could not live and a death we did not die. Jesus paid a debt we could never pay. Yes, our eternal salvation is a free gift to us, because God paid for it with His Son.

Grace surprises us—amazes us—because it is absolutely free and totally undeserved. It is not the justice we expect, or some vague divine mercy we hope for. It is a full and complete pardon from the guilt of our sins, and a new relationship to God that He has made possible. It surprises us because it is not fair. We who deserve eternal death are saved by the One who did not deserve death at all.

Have you been surprised or amazed by grace? Are you now? If so, you have come to grips with the acceptance of something that seems too good to be true—our eternal salvation is simply by grace.

## REVIEW QUESTIONS

1. How would you distinguish between God's justice, mercy, and grace?
2. Compare our common perception of good with God's standard of good.
3. Why can we not be good enough to deserve God's righteousness?
4. What does it mean to be justified, and how can a person be justified?

# SAVED BY GRACE

The Bible could not be clearer—we are saved by grace. There is no other option. How then, can good people disagree about what this means? Because people have different ideas of what grace means. When simple grace is confused with works or merit, it ceases to be grace. Some erroneously teach that to be saved by grace means

- we must believe in Jesus as our Savior and surrender to Him as our Lord.
- we must believe in Jesus as our Savior and also promise to serve Him.
- we must believe in Jesus as Savior and turn from all sins.
- we must believe in Jesus as Savior and give evidence of a changed life.

- we must believe in Jesus as Savior and obey His commandments.
- we must believe in Jesus as Savior and be baptized in water.

All of these state "we must believe in Jesus as Savior," but because they all include some element of merit or performance, they cancel God's grace. No one can be saved if that person is bargaining for or trying to earn God's grace in salvation. Salvation by grace means that all we can do is receive what is given to us. That is where faith comes in. It is the instrument by which we can receive God's gift of eternal salvation.

## GRACE, NOT WORKS

Let's start with the clearest statement about grace and salvation—Ephesians 2:8–9: "For by grace you have been saved through faith, and that not of yourselves; it is the gift of God, not of works, lest anyone should boast."

Here are some simple observations:

1. It is God's grace that saves us;
2. Faith is the means by which we receive that grace;
3. That grace does not originate from within us;
4. The salvation we receive through faith is a gift from God;
5. Salvation by grace through faith excludes any of our good works;
6. Earning salvation by works would allow one to boast, which implies it would steal God's glory.

In the phrase "and that not of yourselves; it is the gift of God," the words *that* and *it* refer to the whole idea of "salvation by the free grace of God through faith." Those words do not refer only to *grace* or *faith* because to do so would require a different form than we see in the original language.[1] This salvation does not originate from within us, for there is nothing in us that can ever deserve God's grace. If we could do something to deserve it, like good works, then as the verse says, we could boast. But think about that—we could boast in the face of God who has given His only Son. In essence we would be saying that God's Son was not enough for our salvation, that the payment God made is not as worthy as what we could do for ourselves. That would be the ultimate insult to God! Imagine the insult you would feel if you sold everything you had to bail your friend out of jail and then that friend boasted that he earned his way out by working hard and behaving well. Your gift would be despised, your benevolence ignored. Now imagine how you would feel if the price you paid was your beloved only son!

This verse affirms our understanding of grace as a totally undeserved and unmerited free gift of God. If we were to work for it, bargain for it, or offer any kind of commitment or obedience for it, it would cease to be grace. That leaves us with only one option—we must believe God for His gift. That is what faith does—it simply receives the gift of eternal life, which God gives to us through the person and work of Jesus, His Son.

So you see how grace requires that we come to God empty-handed. We have nothing to bring, nothing to offer Him for the gift, no way to pay for it. An empty outstretched hand is a good illustration of faith. It has nothing to offer; it can only receive what is given. So it is with our salvation. We receive God's eternal life by simply believing that His promise to us is true—that whoever believes in Jesus Christ has everlasting life. Grace is not something we achieve. It is something we receive.

## WHAT FAITH MEANS

Faith is the noun for the Greek verb "to believe" so that to believe in something is the same as having faith in something. Let's be clear about what it means to believe. To believe something means that we are convinced or persuaded that it is true. We cannot almost believe something. We either believe it or we don't.

Let's say, for example, someone asked you, "Do you believe that five plus fifteen equals twenty?" You could answer (1) "Yes, I believe it"; (2) "No, I don't believe it"; (3) "I'm not sure." If you're not sure, then you don't yet believe that it's true.

Here's another example: you need to pay the rent by midnight or you'll be evicted, but your checking account is empty. I tell you that I've deposited enough funds in your account to pay the rent and that you can go ahead and write a check for the rent. Again, your options are these: (1) You believe me and you write the check; (2) You don't believe me and you don't write the check; (3) You're not sure if you should believe me. If you're not sure, you'd be foolish to write a check, because if I'm not telling the truth the check will bounce and you'll be evicted. The difference lies in how trustworthy you consider my words to be. If you know me enough to be persuaded that I'm trustworthy, you'll believe my words. If you know me to be untrustworthy, you would rightly not believe my words. If you don't know me, you'd be gambling to write a check, and lucky if it didn't bounce.

When it comes to our salvation, we must believe that God's promise is true, that if we simply and only believe in His Son and what He has done for us (died for our sins and rose from the dead), He will give us eternal life. God is perfectly trustworthy and faithful to His promises.

## SIMPLY BELIEVE, ONLY BELIEVE

About two thousand years ago a frightened jailor asked an urgent question: "Sirs, what must I do to be saved?" The apostle Paul answered simply, "Believe on the Lord Jesus Christ, and you will be saved" (Acts 16:30–31). Christians have been arguing about that answer ever since.

Clearly, Paul meant, "Believe in Jesus as the One who can save—the Savior." He refers to Jesus Christ as *Lord*, which implies first of all Jesus' deity, but it is also a title of respect. The jailor used the same Greek word also translated "Sirs" to address Paul and Silas with respect.[2]

The jailor needed *simply* to believe that Jesus is the divine One who could save him. Though not all is known or disclosed in this account, it implies that Paul and Silas told the Philippian jailor about Jesus' provision of salvation through His death and resurrection, which was the message being preached by the Christians.[3] To believe, the jailor must simply accept Jesus' promise as true because of who Jesus is and what He did.

But the jailor also needed *only* to believe. That is, he did not need to do anything else—no good works to do, no rules to keep, no self-improvement to achieve, no promises to make. He did not need to add anything to his faith in God's promise and provision. His simple faith was enough to receive God's gift.

This is where many people go wrong in their understanding of grace. They say that grace must be earned or deserved, therefore faith must include works or prove itself by works. Or they say faith involves total surrender to Jesus as the Master of one's life, or that faith is a commitment we make to God. (These incorrect views of grace will be discussed in the next chapter.) Such views are seen as wrong when we understand the true meaning of grace. We are saved by grace alone through faith alone in Jesus Christ alone.

To be saved by grace means that we believe God's promise of eternal life rather than try to earn it or merit it in some way. Salvation through faith means that we bring nothing to God except our sin because we accept God's promise as true. Grace allows no other options except faith. Being saved simply by grace requires that we receive God's promise simply through faith.

# REVIEW QUESTIONS

1. Explain the nature of a gift. When does something cease to be a gift?

2. Why is salvation available to us only through faith?

3. What are some consequences of relying on our works to save us?

4. How do some contemporary gospel presentations obscure or confuse the biblical concept of salvation by grace through faith?

CHAPTER

# A Maze of Grace

It's a simple concept that eternal life is given absolutely free when one believes God's promise. But it's also controversial. The concept of a free gift is often compromised by a faulty understanding of grace. Some Christians and those of other religions talk about grace, but they distort its meaning. It is important to navigate carefully through this confusing maze of grace. Below are some common misconceptions about grace and how they affect our understanding about eternal salvation. Perhaps you have encountered one of these.

## COSTLY GRACE

Some people speak of costly grace in salvation. It's true that our salvation was costly . . . to God—it required His only son. But some think that our salvation is so wonderful and required so much from God that it must cost us something to enjoy the benefits of eternal life. This leads to the idea that God will not save us eternally unless we commit ourselves to Him, promise to serve Him, surrender our lives to Him, or pay some price. In other words, they think their salvation is costly to *them*. Sometimes it is said that we must make Jesus Christ Lord of our lives or put Him on the "throne" of our lives in order to be saved. While these commitments are expected of believers, requiring this of unbelievers is inconsistent with biblical grace. If God gives us grace only when we meet certain conditions, it ceases to be grace. As we saw, the Bible could not be clearer about the unconditional nature of grace. Grace is not costly; it is absolutely free!

## CHEAP GRACE

The term *cheap grace* is sometimes used in a derogatory way to describe the teaching that grace is free. Just like with *costly grace*, *cheap grace* is not biblical. Grace is neither costly nor cheap; it is free. Those who teach free grace are teaching exactly what the Bible teaches. The Bible does speak of those who despise or abuse God's grace, and in that way they might "cheapen" what value it has in their lives. But those who present eternal salvation as absolutely free are not cheapening grace at all. Grace that is absolutely free does not denigrate God or His salvation. On the contrary, it glorifies God and His incomprehensible and unexplainable love, and it motivates us to the most sincere worship and godliest living. Grace is not costly, cheap, or complicated; it is simple and free.

## EASY-BELIEVISM

The epithet *easy-believism* is also used in a derogatory way against the teaching that salvation is a free gift of God. The intent or implication of this charge is that if we teach salvation by grace alone through faith alone in Christ alone, without requiring commitments or works on our parts to either earn or prove our salvation, then it is too easy, and that will lead to behavior that abuses God's grace. This term is a complete misnomer, because *to believe* is not easy.

- It is not easy to believe that I am a sinner who deserves to be eternally separated from God.
- It is not easy to believe that I can do nothing to save myself from eternal condemnation.
- It is not easy to believe that God became a man, lived a perfect life, was killed anyway, and then rose from the dead.
- It is not easy to believe that a life given two thousand years ago will provide a payment for my sins today.
- It is not easy to believe that God loves me so much and is so generous that He will give me eternal life as a free gift.

It is not *easy* to believe! But it is *simple* to believe, because there is only one condition—believe in God's gracious provision and promise.

## ASSISTED GRACE

Some religions speak often of grace, but only as God's assistance to our own efforts. It is considered as a spiritual boost or addition to our good works or devotion. Roman Catholicism, for example, teaches that God confers His grace on those who keep the seven sacraments—baptism, Eucharist, penance, confirmation, marriage, holy orders, anointing of the sick. The teaching goes that faith alone in God's promise of salvation cannot save anyone. In this view, since keeping the sacraments is necessary for salvation, and the sacraments are things that must be done, the implication is that God's grace is not enough to save us. We must cooperate with Him by our good works, and only then will He "give" us the grace needed for salvation. You can see how this is not grace at all, because it must be earned by our works.

## INSUFFICIENT GRACE

Some religions speak favorably about grace but they mean that it is only God's favor or kindness. That is how the Jehovah's Witnesses understand and translate grace. God is kind and favorable to us and will reward our works and obedience with salvation. Again, however, grace is not grace if it must be attained by our performance. The Church of Jesus Christ of Latter Day Saints (Mormonism) views grace like a ladder lowered into a hole to allow people to climb out by their own efforts. In their view, grace is an opportunity or ability that allows us to save ourselves. Though grace *is* God's kindness to us, it is so much more. It is God's *total* provision for our need, not just a helping hand. His grace is sufficient to meet any need we have, starting with salvation.

## LICENTIOUS GRACE

A licentious view of grace teaches that since grace is absolutely free, once saved we can do whatever we wish with no consequences—it is a license to sin. This is a perversion of the biblical concept of free grace. Yes, grace is absolutely free, and yes, there is nothing we can do that will undo our eternal standing before God. If we cannot be saved by what we do, we cannot be lost by what we do (or don't do). But the Bible teaches that grace brings responsibility and calls for obedience. When we do not live responsibly or obediently, there are negative consequences in this life and the next (see chapter 9). Believers are no longer under the Old Testament Law, but in the New Testament we have "the law of Christ" and many commands related to godly living.

Those who truly understand and appreciate the grace that saved them will not want to exploit that grace, but they will be motivated to live a life that honors God. Grace is a higher principle to live by, which, when properly understood and applied, helps us live a godly life. The Bible also admonishes us not to use our freedom as a license to sin, but to serve God and help others.[1] The fact that we are so admonished shows that the abuse of God's grace is a reality for some and a possibility for all.

## REPENTANCE AND GRACE

The word *repentance* is very often misused by people in explaining the condition for salvation. The Greek word for *repentance* is formed from two words that mean "afterthought" or "to change the mind." It signifies an inner change, a change of mind or heart, which should lead to an outward change. When we speak of repentance associated with salvation, it is a general way of describing the change of mind that occurs when one believes the gospel. The unsaved man or woman goes from not realizing his or her need to realizing that need, or from not understanding God's provision and promise of eternal life to understanding and accepting it. In this sense the meaning of repentance coincides with faith as the condition for salvation. With this use of repentance, there is no contradiction of God's free grace. But many people wrongly believe that salvation comes only after one turns from all one's sins, even though there is no support for defining repentance in terms of outward conduct. To the contrary, repentance as an inner change of heart is demonstrated by the many uses of the word in the New Testament. When John the Baptist, for example, tells the Pharisees to "bear fruits worthy of repentance,"[2] we see the difference between inner repentance and the outer conduct resulting from it. If repentance is understood as a change in conduct or turning from sins *for* salvation, it corrupts the free grace of God.

## BAPTISM AND GRACE

There are also those who require baptism in order to be saved. If this were true, then grace would be conditioned on a physical act. Baptism is important in that it identifies someone as a Christian, that is, someone saved by grace. It is an important outward symbol of a spiritual reality. But as such, it is commanded subsequent to salvation, not as a condition for salvation.[3] If baptism were a condition required for salvation, it would compromise free grace.

## WORKS AND GRACE

A broad category of people maintain that the grace that saves is dependent on works of some kind. Some say that grace is given only to those who obey God or promise to obey. We who profess free grace call this "frontloading" the gospel. Others say that grace is really given only to those who prove they are Christians by their works; we call this "backloading" the gospel. Some try to argue that the works involved are not works motivated by our sinful nature (to earn salvation), but by the Spirit's work in us. But when the Bible disqualifies works as a condition for salvation, it does not make any such distinction. Works as a condition for salvation are dismissed summarily. The importance of good works for the Christian life will be discussed in chapter 8.

Many people have taken the principle of simple grace and have complicated, confused, and corrupted it so that it is no longer what the Bible teaches. We want to keep grace consistent with the Bible's teaching that it is an absolutely free gift. Salvation is simply by grace through faith. That means it is a free gift that someone must merely accept. Free grace is a simple concept, so simple many people miss it. Yet it is so profound that only God can accomplish it. Salvation by grace reserves the glory for God instead of us. In our natural human aversion to grace, we want to do something to earn our salvation. This appeals to our pride of accomplishment or makes us feel worthy. But God gives salvation as a free gift to reserve the glory exclusively for Himself, where it belongs.

## REVIEW QUESTIONS

1. How would you refute the terms *costly grace, cheap grace,* and *easy-believism*?

2. Does salvation by grace allow for any assistance or contribution on our parts? Explain.

3. Explain how a misunderstanding of repentance can contradict salvation by grace.

4. What is the role of baptism when it comes to salvation?

# SECURED BY GRACE

You are not grounded in grace if you do not believe in the security of your salvation. How can I make that blunt statement? Because if your relationship with God is not secure, not grounded firmly in His unconditional promise, then it is left to your imperfect performance, which is no basis for eternal security.

Security means that our eternal salvation will never be lost or forfeited because of what we do or do not do. *Never.* If we cannot be saved by what we do or do not do, then we cannot lose our salvation by what we do or do not do.

Those who understand grace and its implications will be confident of their eternal security. Since our salvation is grounded in God's promise and not in our performance, since it is a free undeserved gift and not something we must earn, then we are secure. God's promise is sure and He cannot lie. Romans 3:4 says, "Let God be true but every man a liar." In 2 Timothy 2:13 we read, "If we are faithless,

He remains faithful; He cannot deny Himself." In other words, even if we were to deny our relationship to Jesus Christ (as the disciple Peter did), God is faithful to His promise to give us His salvation.

## A WIDESPREAD PROBLEM

There are good people everywhere, perhaps good Christians, who do not believe they are saved forever. They believe that their salvation can be lost. This belief affects them in different ways. Some may not be troubled by that thought at all, while others live in fear and doubt about their eternal future. The possibility of being forever separated from God haunts them from deep inside, which may cause them to live uprightly, serve in church, or do whatever is necessary to prove to themselves and to others that they are saved. Yet doubts remain because performance is always imperfect.

Those who believe that salvation can be lost often resent the teaching that it cannot be lost. I've seen a lot of emotion generated by this subject. The argument against eternal security is usually framed in this way: "If you teach that we cannot lose our salvation, then Christians will do whatever they want. They will have a license to sin." I have found that those who argue this way are usually good people with sincere motives who want to see Christians live godly lives.

The view that believers cannot lose their salvation is sometimes referred to as "Once saved always saved." While that is an accurate description, it has been used derogatorily by so many for so long that it elicits more emotional response than reason. Let us think beyond pejorative labels. If, for example, our eternal salvation can be lost, some big questions are raised:

- What sins will cause a man to lose his salvation? Where is the definitive list in the Bible?

- How does a woman know when she has lost her salvation?

- How does a man get saved all over again? Should he only believe? Believe what, because he has already believed in Christ as Savior if he was saved at all. Should he turn from his sins? Then salvation comes through something other than faith alone in Christ alone.

- How can a woman who does not believe in eternal security share the gospel with confidence? Her message must be "Jesus will save you eternally . . . maybe."

- How can a man grow confidently in his fellowship with God when he is not sure that his relationship to Him is secure to begin with?

You can see the problems that are created by the view that salvation can be lost. That view instead seems to create many more problems than the supposed problems created by eternal security. The greatest challenge for we who believe in eternal security is to explain some of the Bible passages that appear to teach that Christians can lose their salvation. We will not be able to address each of those passages, but we can lay a framework that will help us interpret them.

## THE GRACE SOLUTION

The gospel of grace answers the above list of questions simply: eternal salvation is free and unconditional, so it cannot be lost. If it could be lost, it would not be called *eternal*. The reason we can affirm our eternal security is not presumption or pride, but confidence in God's gracious promise. We have already seen how the book of Romans establishes that salvation is by grace alone through faith alone in Jesus Christ. Unconditional, undeserved grace is exactly that. It may be hard to believe, but God *really is* that good!

To make the point that grace is undeserved and must therefore be received through faith alone, Romans 4:3 and Galatians 3:6 both quote Genesis 15:6: "Abraham believed God, and it was accounted to him for righteousness." These quotations look back to Abraham and the promise God made to him of a coming Offspring who would bless the world and whom we now know is Jesus Christ. In both cases Paul is showing that salvation must be by grace through faith in that Savior just as it was for Abraham. If it is through faith and not works, then the promise is sure because it depends on God's faithfulness, not ours. That is the point of Romans 4:16: "Therefore it is of faith that it might be according to grace, so that the promise might be sure to all the seed, not only to those who are of the law, but also to those who are of the faith of Abraham, who is the father of us all."[1]

If the promise depended on Abraham's performance, there would be no nation of Israel and no Messiah, and no fulfillment of God's promised blessing through them. Israel's history is a story of rebellion and sin. Yet God has promised that "all Israel *will be saved*" in a future day of restoration because He will be faithful to His promises[2]—*He cannot deny Himself!* Likewise, God has promised eternal life to all who believe like Abraham. That promise does not depend on our performance but on Jesus Christ's performance. Jesus did the perfect and all-sufficient work.

## THE MOUNTAINTOP OF GRACE

The argument for eternal security climaxes in Romans 8 as Paul explains the results of justification and sanctification by grace through faith. A full explanation of the chapter is unnecessary to appreciate the main points. Consider how eternal security is conveyed by the truths listed in this summary of key verses.

- 8:15–16: We are adopted into God's family with God as our Father.
- 8:17: We are heirs of God—recipients of His promise.
- 8:23: We have the Holy Spirit as our firstfruits, or guarantee of the future redemption of our bodies.
- 8:28: All of life's experiences will not prevent God's purpose for us, but will work for our good to accomplish His purpose for us.
- 8:29: God's unalterable purpose is that all whom He sovereignly determined will be conformed to the image of His Son.
- 8:30: All those God selected will be glorified, with no exceptions.

- 8:31: Since God is on our side, nothing can prevail against us to thwart His purpose of our glorification.

- 8:32: Since God gave us the greatest gift of His Son to save us, He will also give us all the other things that will bring us final glorification.

- 8:33: Since God has chosen us and declared us righteous, no one can reverse that with any charge of guilt.

- 8:34: Since God has accepted the sacrifice of His Son for us, and Jesus intercedes for us, nothing can condemn us.

- 8:35–39: Nothing and no one can separate us from God's unconditional love.

All these assurances of our eternal security depend on what God has done, not on our performance.

## GOD'S DOUBLE GRIP

We can look also to the gospel of John for assurances of our eternal security. Every promise of eternal salvation in John, in fact, states or implies a life given to us that is . . . *eternal!* When God makes a promise to us like John 3:16, "that whoever believes in [Jesus] should not perish but have everlasting life," He will keep it. He attaches no conditions for us beyond believing that this promise is true for us. In John 6:37 Jesus says, "All that the Father gives Me will come to Me, and the one who comes to Me I will by no means cast out." The word *All* means no exceptions. If Jesus will not cast out anyone, then there is nothing any believer can do to make Him cast that believer out.

One passage, John 10:27–30, is especially assuring.

> My sheep hear My voice, and I know them, and they follow Me.
>
> And I give them eternal life, and they shall never perish; neither shall anyone snatch them out of My hand. My Father, who has given them to Me, is greater than all; and no one is able to snatch them out of My Father's hand.
>
> I and My Father are one.

In this passage we are told that the believer is firmly in Christ's hand and Christ is firmly in His Father's hand. This divine double grip conveys our preservation for all eternity. Again it is not *us* holding on to Him, but *Him* holding on to us that keeps us securely saved.

A father and young son were crossing a busy street. The father grabbed his son's tiny hand and told him to hold on tightly. When they reached the other side of the street, the boy said, "I held on tight didn't I, Dad?" "Yes," the Dad replied, "but I held on first!" If salvation depended on our grip, we would eventually let go. Only God can guarantee our eternal future with Him.

## AND MORE ARGUMENTS

Many other lines of argument as well support eternal security. Consider these truths from Scripture:

- Since we are born again spiritually (literally, *born from above*), we cannot be unborn (John 1:12–13; 3:3–6).

- Since we are sealed by the Holy Spirit, which means He guarantees our eternal future (2 Cor. 1:22; Eph. 1:13–14; 4:30), that seal cannot be broken until its purpose has been attained.

- Since we are baptized into Christ and united with Him, we cannot be un-baptized or severed from Him (Rom. 6:3–5; 1 Cor. 12:13).

- Since God is a good heavenly Father, He would never kick us out of His family, though He may discipline us (Heb. 12:5–7).

- Since all of our sins—past, present, future—are forgiven by Jesus Christ and His eternally sufficient sacrifice, there is no sin that can cause us to lose our relationship to Him (Col. 2:13–14; Heb. 10:12–14).

- Since we have the intercessory prayers of Jesus Christ and His advocacy when we sin, we are guaranteed that our salvation will be completed eternally (John 17:9–12, 24; Heb. 7:25; 1 John 2:1).

- Since the Bible speaks of salvation in the passive voice (we "have been saved"), which indicates that the primary Actor is God, our salvation is based upon His work, not ours (Eph. 2:5, 8; 2 Thess. 2:10; 1 Tim. 2:4).

- Since the Bible demonstrates by example (Abraham, David, Israel) and by precept that God is faithful to His eternal promises even when we are not faithful in our obedience, all of His eternal promises to us will be fulfilled in spite of our behavior (Ps. 89:30–37; Rom. 3:3–4; 4:16; 2 Tim. 2:13).

## WHAT ABOUT THOSE OTHER PASSAGES?

Those who do not believe in eternal security cite a number of Bible passages as evidence that salvation can be lost. There are too many to address here, but when interpreted consistently and correctly, each of the selected passages below can be understood in a way that harmonizes with eternal security. Here are some helpful tips for interpreting these passages:

- First, they must be interpreted in accord with the context that considers the spiritual state of the readers and the purpose of the author.[3]

- Second, they must be consistent with the overarching plan of God to bless us eternally by His grace (Rom. 4:16; Eph. 1:3–14).

- Third, they must harmonize with the consistent teaching of justification by grace through faith alone apart from works or any other merit.[4]

- Fourth, some of these passages are referring to loss of reward, not loss of eternal life (for example, 1 Cor. 3:11–15; 9:24–27).

- Fifth, some of these passages refer to God's discipline of believers in this life (for example, Pss. 32:3–4; 51:7–13; 1 Cor. 11:30).

- Sixth, some of these passages relate to the conditions and consequences of discipleship, not salvation from hell (for example, Luke 9:23–26; 14:26; John 15:6).

Too often Christians will read these questionable passages through the interpretive lens of saved/unsaved or heaven/hell. You can see that there are other options that render a more accurate and meaningful interpretation.

## A License to Sin?

As mentioned earlier, a common objection to the doctrine of eternal security is that it is a convenient excuse to sin. "After all," the objector would say, "if a man is guaranteed eternal life, then he can do whatever he wants without fear of consequence." But this argument is weak for a number of reasons.

- First, an argument from a hypothetical or an observed experience does not determine the truthfulness of a belief.
- Second, while some who hold to eternal security may sin and excuse it, those who reject eternal security may do the same.
- Third, the nature of salvation by grace is that it teaches the believer to deny ungodliness and to live for God (Titus 2:11–12).

- Fourth, new birth gives a person a new capacity for spiritual things, a new relationship with God, a new freedom not to sin, a new life, and a new perspective and orientation (Rom. 6; Eph. 2:1; 2 Cor. 5:17).

- Fifth, the Bible teaches that there are severe consequences and loss of rewards for believers who live sinfully (1 Cor. 3:12–15; 5:5; 9:27; 2 Cor. 5:10), which is a good motivation to live a godly life.

Do some people use eternal security as an excuse to live carelessly and sin recklessly? I'm sure they do. Jude wrote about "ungodly men, who turn the grace of our God into lewdness and deny the only Lord God and our Lord Jesus Christ" (Jude 4). Paul evidently encountered people who had adopted such reasoning and rejected it (Rom. 6:1–2, 15). While I know that such Christians exist, I cannot recall ever meeting one who uses eternal security as an excuse to sin. On the contrary, I've met many people who are so amazed by the grace that saved them and keeps them saved that they have gratefully surrendered their lives to God's service. Doing so is, after all, the only appropriate response to grace.

## SAME OLD PROBLEM

The controversy about eternal security is nothing new. It is the same basic issue behind the problem that Paul confronted when he wrote his letter to the Galatians. In brief, Paul had preached the gospel of grace to the Galatians and they were saved, but now they were beginning to abandon that gospel for another (Gal. 1:6–7). Soon after he left them, other teachers came and taught that it was not enough to simply believe in Jesus Christ as their Savior. They taught that the Galatian Christians needed to get back under the Jewish Law to finish their salvation or remain saved. So by implication they taught them that they had to keep their salvation by works or by obeying the Law (5:1–12).

In his letter to the Galatians, Paul shows them the inconsistencies of that view.

- It is not consistent with the gospel of grace that he had taught them (1:6–10).

- It is not consistent with Paul's testimony. He was converted out of Judaism and received the gospel of grace by revelation (1:1–24); he would not circumcise Titus (2:1–5); he was called to preach grace to the Gentiles (2:6–10); he had confronted Peter for pressuring Gentiles to live under the Law as Jews (2:11–21).

- It is not consistent with how the Galatians had received the Holy Spirit at salvation, that is, through faith (3:1–5).

- It is not consistent with how Abraham was saved through faith alone and received God's promises through faith alone (3:6–9).

- It is not consistent with the purpose of the Law, which was given not to save us but to bring us to Christ for salvation (3:10–25).

- It is not consistent with the Galatians' new position as free sons, not slaves (3:2–4:7; 4:21–31).

- It is not consistent with their early receptivity and hospitality toward Paul and his message (4:8–20).

- It is not consistent with the liberty that had set them free from being obligated to obey the Law (5:1–15).

- It is not consistent with walking in the Spirit and the Spirit-controlled life (5:16–26).

In the words of the apostle, to go back to relying on one's performance instead of Christ's finished work is to turn away from Christ Himself (1:6), is to "set aside the grace of God" (2:21a), to make Christ's death in vain (2:21b), not to obey the truth (3:1; 5:7), return to bondage (4:9; 5:1), become obligated to keep all the Law perfectly (5:3), be estranged from Christ (5:4), fall from the grace that gives us full assurance of God's acceptance (5:4), and become susceptible to the lusts of the flesh (5:16–26). The danger facing the Galatians then, and those who rely on their works to keep their salvation now, is the need to perform perfectly in order to keep God pleased. Paul's words in Galatians teach us why that is impossible and totally unnecessary because we are accepted by God on the basis of the grace that comes from Jesus Christ received through faith.

Today those who do not believe in eternal security usually do not teach that the Christian must keep the Old Testament Law. But when they teach that certain sins or a sinful lifestyle can forfeit salvation, the problem is the same as the one Paul confronted in the Galatian church—salvation depends on performance instead of God's promise.

Eternal security is not an excuse to sin. It is an amazing insight into the depths of God's love and commitment to us, and an extension of the same grace that saved us in the first place. It is inconsistent and even contradictory to believe that we are saved freely but kept saved by our own efforts. The extraordinary, unexpected, and undeserved blessing of grace is that it always exceeds our sin: "But where sin abounded, grace abounded much more" (Rom. 5:20). It is simply amazing grace!

## REVIEW QUESTIONS

1. What are some potential spiritual consequences for not believing that salvation is eternally secure?

2. How do the stories of Abraham and Israel reinforce the concept of eternal security for the believer?

3. In what ways can we approach those Bible passages used by some to claim that salvation is not eternally secure?

4. How would you answer the objection that eternal security is a license to sin?

CHAPTER

# ASSURED BY GRACE

We have seen that eternal security is the objective truth that we are related to God forever. Assurance is the subjective realization or experience of that truth. Our eternal security cannot change; our assurance can.

## AN EPIDEMIC OF DOUBT

The lack of assurance is a pervasive problem in the world and in the church, and I believe it is of crisis proportion. If misunderstanding eternal security is a big problem among Christians, you can see how assurance is also. I'm convinced that in just about every church there are people who are not sure they are saved, and yet many of them are Christians. Many or even most Christians at one time or another have struggled with knowing for sure they are saved. I did, and as a pastor I continually met others who did. I have even met seminary students who were not sure they were saved. Imagine that—people studying so they can bring good news and hope to others, but they themselves do not know if they are Christians!

I've asked many people this question: "If you were to die and stand before God and He were to ask you, 'Why should I let you into My heaven?' what would you answer?" Some typical answers are, "I am a pretty good person," "I try to be good," "I try to keep the Bible's commandments," "I've tried to do the best I can." Then my next question is, "How do you know when you're good enough or have done enough?" From there it's easy to show them that they cannot be sure about their eternal destiny based on their own idea of goodness or their performance. That's because there's always somebody who is better than them, and besides God's standard for heaven is perfection.

With so many views of the gospel being preached, it's no wonder so many believers are confused and in doubt about their salvation. But there are other reasons people stumble into doubt.

## DOUBTS ABOUT DOUBTS

Some Christians unfortunately perpetuate the lack of assurance by teaching that doubts are good. They say doubts make us examine our lives to see if our salvation is genuine. But that is an exercise in futility because no life is perfect and no one's judgment is flawless.

One passage used to argue that doubts are good is 2 Corinthians 13:5, which says, "Examine yourselves as to whether you are in the faith. Test yourselves. Do you not know yourselves, that Jesus

Christ is in you?—unless indeed you are disqualified." But this does not teach that Christians should question their salvation. In the context, Paul is defending his authenticity as an apostle against the attacks of the false apostles.[1] He is saying, "Don't examine *my* authenticity; examine *yours!*" One of the greatest proofs that Paul is a true apostle preaching the true gospel is the Corinthians themselves. If they are saved and know that Christ is in them, then Paul is authentic because he is the one who preached Christ to them. Paul assumes that they do, indeed, know that Christ is in them.

Sometimes doubt is built into a church's tradition and culture. Preachers harangue churchgoers, causing them to question whether they are really saved. "Do you give enough, witness enough, attend church enough, pray enough?" and so on. "Real Christians would give more, witness more, attend church more, pray more," they say. Then the people are constantly invited to "Get right with God," which in some cloudy way implies that they need to *really* be saved. In some church traditions a whole "revivalistic" and "evangelistic" industry has resulted from getting saved people to feel unsaved so that they can be "truly" saved or saved again.

No healthy relationship can be built on doubt and uncertainty. That is true in human relationships and in our relationship with God. Doubts inhibit confidence, intimacy, and maturity. Suppose two parents have a young daughter. When she does what they tell her, they assure her with the words "That's our daughter!" When she disobeys, they tell her, "I don't think you're our daughter, because you didn't do what we said." Is that a healthy environment for growth? How could it be? That daughter is not grounded in unconditional love and acceptance, which undermines her motivation to grow and to please the parents. Sooner or later she'll probably tire of such fickle conditional love and may give up trying to please her parents altogether. The same sad outcome occurs for many who live with doubts about their salvation because they are in a religious system that makes God's grace and salvation conditional.

I'm strongly convinced that those who doubt their salvation do not have a solid foundation for further Christian growth. They are not grounded in grace. Their forward look toward growth and maturity is constantly interrupted by their backward glance to check if they are really saved. No one can go forward as God wants when that person is looking backward. Or to use an analogy, no one can mature as a child of God when that person wonders if he or she really is His child at all.

## WHY PEOPLE DOUBT

People may have doubts about their eternal salvation for a number of reasons.

One obvious reason is that it's possible that they may have never believed the gospel of grace. Many people believe in a false or faulty gospel or respond to an emotional appeal at church, or to the feeling that God is speaking to them about something. They may have thought that joining a church meant they were saved, but they have nagging doubts whether that did it. These people have never really understood the gospel message—that we are sinners who need to be saved, and that Jesus Christ is God's Son, who died to pay the penalty for our sin and then rose from the dead and promises us eternal life if we believe Him for it.

People can also be filled with doubts if they believed the gospel at one time, but later fell into false teaching. They may be misled to believe that they lose their salvation because of sin, not feeling saved, not going to church, or any number of things.

Some believers will doubt their salvation because they fall into sin and their conscience is confused or condemning them. They mistake the conviction of sin and the effects of guilt with the loss of salvation.

When believers experience severe trials, it could cause them to wonder if God still loves and accepts them. This is why the Bible reassures us that no bad thing that happens to us can separate us from God's love.[2]

People with an introspective or emotional personality often have trouble with their assurance of salvation. They are prone to depend too much on feelings so that they question themselves.

Christians who have been lied to or betrayed by others can easily have problems with assurance. They have issues of trust that are projected onto God, even though He is totally trustworthy. For them, it is just plain difficult to believe someone, even God.

When the emphasis is on feelings, some Christians may not feel the indwelling presence of the Holy Spirit. Let's face it—there are bad days when everything feels bad. Sickness, fatigue, pressure, criticism, or a spoiled piece of fish can disrupt our internal mechanisms physically, emotionally, psychologically, and spiritually.

Some Christians belong to churches or groups that so emphasize the doctrines of God's predestination and election that they may wonder if they are one of God's elect or chosen ones. This is especially true when they are taught that professing Christians can only know for sure when they die because they must persevere to the end of their lives in faith and good works. No one can know now if he or she will be living faithfully at the time of death, so by default no one can know that he or she is saved.

How my heart breaks for people who have fallen into these errors! How much more is God's heart broken by those who doubt His unconditional love. How can their doubts about salvation be dispelled? How can they live and rejoice in freedom from their uncertainty and be assured that they belong to God forever? It's simply by grace.

## CAN WE KNOW FOR SURE?

In spite of the teaching that we cannot know for sure we are saved or that doubts are good and normal for the Christian, we have to deal with the biblical data. There is no doubt (the pun may be intended!) that New Testament authors knew they were saved. Just read the introduction to some of the epistles and see how they referred to themselves. In Romans 1:1, for example, we read, "Paul, a bondservant of Jesus Christ, called to be an apostle, separated to the gospel of God." No uncertainty there! Paul knew that if he were to die he would immediately pass into the presence of the Lord. "We are confident, yes, well pleased rather to be absent from the body and to be present with the Lord" (2 Cor. 5:8). No uncertainty there either! We get the same certainty from James (James 1:1), Peter (1 Peter. 1:1; 2 Peter 1:1), Jude (Jude 1), and John. Let's talk more about John.

The apostle John wrote these words in 1 John 5:11–13:

> And this is the testimony: that God has given us
> eternal life, and this life is in His Son. He who has
> the Son has life; he who does not have the Son of
> God does not have life. These things I have written
> to you who believe in the name of the Son of God,
> that you may know that you have eternal life, and
> that you may continue to believe in the name of the
> Son of God.

John tells his readers that if they have Jesus Christ, they have eternal life. Since they have believed in Jesus they should *know* that they have eternal life. It is a simple statement of fact. All people born into the family of God through faith in Jesus Christ should know that they have eternal life.

John and the other New Testament authors knew their readers were saved, as evidenced by the terms they use for them: *brothers, holy brothers, beloved of God, babes in Christ, saints, heirs of God, church of God, elect*, and so on. They sometimes greet them in the name of "God our Father" (1 Thess. 1:1; 2 Thess. 1:1), "God our Savior" (1 Tim. 1:1), "Jesus Christ our Lord" or "our Lord Jesus Christ"

(1 Cor. 1:2; 2 Cor. 1:2; 1 Peter 1:3). Sometimes the authors commend their readers for their faith and obedience (Rom. 6:17; Col. 1:4; 1 Thess. 1:3). The point is, if we can find just *one* instance in which any of their readers are considered to be saved, or consider themselves saved, then it is possible for them to know that they are saved. If this were not true, the epistles would be like shots fired randomly, hoping to hit a target—the saved. The full force and responsibility conveyed by the various authors' admonitions are realized only by those who know they are saved.

I have heard some object that it's presumptuous to assume you are saved. They argue that only God can know and only God needs to know. But the presumption is in those who would say such a thing in light of a passage like 1 John 5:1–13. If God wants us to know we are saved, then it is presumptuous *not* to know. If God made us a promise to be believed, then it is presumptuous not to take God at His Word! Who are we to say His promise cannot be true for us? His word is true as stated. God thinks that we should know and that we need to know!

## DISPELLING THE DOUBTS

The gospel of John is also important in our discussion of assurance because John wrote it for a specific purpose: "And truly Jesus did many other signs in the presence of His disciples, which are not written in this book; but these are written that you may believe that Jesus is the Christ, the Son of God, and that believing you may have life in His name" (John 20:30–31).

John wrote so that his readers would believe in Jesus and receive eternal life. If no one could be sure about that, would John have ever realized his purpose? To accomplish his purpose he repeatedly records the promises of God. The best known is in John 3:16: "For God so loved the world that He gave His only begotten Son, that whoever believes in Him should not perish but have everlasting life."

The promise of God's gift of eternal life could not be more simple; believe in His Son, Jesus, and you will have everlasting life. You either believe this or you do not.[3]

Another good passage for John's purpose is John 5:24: "Most assuredly, I say to you, he who hears My word and believes in Him who sent Me has everlasting life, and shall not come into judgment, but has passed from death into life."

Again, the promise is simple and sure. If you believe in Christ, you will not come into judgment (for your sins, including unbelief), but will pass from death to life, from being separated from God to being born into His family. There is no middle ground of uncertainty.

One more passage from John is 6:47: "Most assuredly, I say to you, he who believes in Me has everlasting life." Nothing new here, only the simplest reiteration of God's promise. Believe and you will have everlasting (eternal) life.

## ARE *YOU* SURE?

Now we see that the problem of assurance cannot be with God's Word, its purpose, clarity, or simplicity. The problem can only be with us who hear it. Do we believe it or not? Or better stated, do we believe *Him* or not? Based on the Word of God we know that if we believe in Jesus Christ as our Savior, then we can know that we have eternal life. That really should settle it. There is no higher authority than God's Word.

Although I'd heard these promises most of my childhood, I don't recall that anyone ever challenged me to believe that they were true for me personally. I thought they were true for the world in some general and cosmic way. But later as a teenager with a heart hungry for truth, someone challenged me to read them again and personally appropriate (believe) the promises. They sounded true, and I believed them. But I read other literature and listened to other people who had different views about how to have eternal life. Soon I became confused. Was I sorry enough for my sins? Had I turned from all of my sins? Did I make Jesus Christ the Master of all of my life? Had I promised to love, obey, and serve Him? And the list would keep growing. Almost immediately after I had believed, I became confused. *Could these other conditions be necessary for eternal life?* I thought. *If so, am I really saved?*

I remember the time I settled my doubts once and for all. Up to that point if people asked me if I was a Christian I would say, "I don't know." It seemed presumptuous and arrogant to say "Yes" as if I had done all the things others said I needed to do. But one evening after a Christian concert, I went up to tell one of the group how much I enjoyed their music. This fellow grabbed my hand looked me in the eye and said, "Charlie, are you a Christian?" In the second it took to answer, I remember thinking how ridiculous it is to have doubts about God's simple promise of eternal life. Evidently this guy knew he was saved and he expected me to know—*God* expected me to know! "Yes," I said. And I have never had to answer otherwise since.

The way I understand the Bible, anyone who is a true Christian would at some point have had to believe God's promise of eternal life, because that's what it means to become a Christian, a *believer*. Some people have never had to look back or deal with doubts about their salvation. They believed God's promise and that settled it. Others believed but later got confused. Some find their way out of the fog, others live there—miserably.

But the truth we must not miss is this: God wants us to know we are saved and it pleases Him when we believe His promise because it glorifies His love, grace, and faithfulness. He really is that good, that loving, that giving, and He wants to show us. But He cannot do so if we doubt His promise. If eternal life depended on our works, our commitment, or our faithfulness, we would rightfully wonder if we had done enough, committed enough, or been faithful enough. Doubt is the inevitable outcome when we take our eyes off of God and His promise through Jesus Christ. If we believe in the Lord Jesus Christ, we have eternal life.

You can be sure of that.

It's a tragedy that so many Christians suffer the consequences of no assurance. They cannot go forward, because they're always looking backward, wondering if they were really saved. Their witness is timid because they don't really believe God's promise themselves. Their ministry is constantly undermined by a shaky foundation of uncertainty.

But to those who have accepted God's promises as sure, there is rejoicing. We have been saved; we are saved; we are His forever—simply by grace!

## REVIEW QUESTIONS

1. What are some reasons Christians doubt their salvation?
2. Is it proud or presumptuous to claim that you are sure of your salvation? Explain.
3. What Bible passages would you use to help those who doubt their salvation?
4. Explain how you can or did settle doubts about your own salvation.

# Chapter 8

# Grace and Good Works

So far we've focused our discussion on what is required to obtain eternal life, to keep eternal life, and to be sure you have eternal life. According to grace, our human effort, good works, and sincere commitments are irrelevant to receiving eternal life because it all depends on God's efforts, His good works, and His commitments. In other words, He did it all. It is simply by His grace.

We saw that Romans 3:20 says, "By the deeds of the law no flesh will be justified in His sight, for by the law is the knowledge of sin." And Romans 4:4–5 says faith, not works is the only requirement for salvation: "Now to him who works, the wages are not counted as grace but as debt. But to him who does not work but believes on Him who justifies the ungodly, his faith is accounted for righteousness."

So when it comes to salvation, good works are a bad idea. But if we cannot be saved by the works or good things that we do, how do good works fit in? We know the Bible says a lot about doing good works and godly living. How are they important?

## GOOD WORKS ARE A GOOD IDEA

Good works are not a requirement for salvation; they are to be a result of salvation. It is crucial to keep this order in mind. The experience of God's saving grace should always result in good works. When we have experienced the free gift of salvation, we learn to live a life that is pleasing to God. Grace guides us into godliness, not the other way around. "For the grace of God that brings salvation has appeared to all men, teaching us that, denying ungodliness and worldly lusts, we should live soberly, righteously, and godly in the present age" (Titus 2:11–12).

Because works are not necessary for salvation, we must not conclude that they are not important to God. Good works *after salvation* are a good idea because they are God's idea. Here is why good works are important:

*Good works are God's purpose.* We looked at Ephesians 2:8–9, which says that we are saved by grace through faith and not by works. But the next verse tells us God's purpose in our salvation: "For we are His workmanship, created in Christ Jesus for good works, which God prepared beforehand that we should walk in them" (Eph. 2:10).

It is God's preordained purpose that we who have believed live according to good works. That is why He has made us new creations in Jesus Christ.

*Good works are commanded by God.* The Bible does command many good works—too many to cite ("Love one another" should be the first one that comes to mind). But they are commands to *Christians* in light of salvation not to unbelievers as conditions for salvation. To know that God commands these things should be enough to see their importance and obey.

*Good works glorify God.* To glorify God is to give Him what He is due, to honor Him, to magnify Him. When Jesus did a good work or a miracle, the Bible often says that the people glorified God.[1] When we do good works, we glorify God or cause others to glorify God.[2]

*Good works help believers and unbelievers.* This is obvious but must be said. Our good works can feed the hungry, help the sick, or show mercy to those in need.

So while good works are never a *requirement* for salvation, they are an expected *result* of salvation. They are not a *condition* for salvation, but a *consequence* of salvation. Having stated that, we must be careful in thinking we can quantify someone's good works in a measurable or verifiable way. After all, non-Christians and even atheists do good works, and what we might assume is a good work done by a Christian might not be considered so by God. Things that appear to be good works can come from bad motives.

## THE MOTIVATION TO DO GOOD WORKS

Those who understand and experience God's grace have the greatest motivation to do good works as they seek to please God.

The biblical motivation for good works is not to gain salvation or to stay out of hell, but to show love and gratitude toward the God who gave His Son so that we could have the free gift of eternal life. Grace is the purest motivation for a life of good works.

When we look at some of Paul's epistles, we see that his admonitions to good conduct follow his explanations about the blessings we have in Christ through grace. This is most evident in Romans, where, before our practical conduct is even discussed, we read eleven chapters about how God has blessed us. Paul waits until 12:1 to tell us how we can respond to grace. "I beseech you therefore, brethren, by the mercies of God, that you present your bodies a living sacrifice, holy, acceptable to God, which is your reasonable service."

The word *therefore* in "I beseech you therefore, brethren, by the mercies of God" indicates that Paul is drawing a general conclusion from all of his theological teaching about grace in chapters 1–11. In other words, since we are saved, sanctified, secured, and selected by God's grace, here is how we can respond—by offering ourselves totally to Him in order to serve Him. But what does that mean? In his exhortations to godly conduct, Paul explains in chapters 12–16 of Romans what it means to serve God sacrificially.

The sequence in Romans is also found in other epistles: God's blessings prompt good behavior; theological truth informs practical conduct; belief leads to behavior; grace motivates grateful living. We see this progression in Galatians 1–4 to 5–6; Ephesians 1–3 to 4–6; and Colossians 1–2 to 3–4, where Paul is teaching that works flow out of salvation. Works are not required before salvation.

## ONLY TWO RELIGIONS

By now you should understand what makes grace so simple and amazing and why biblical Christianity is different from all the other religions of the world. All other religions require something that needs to be done or followed before one can be saved or enjoy an eternal reward in the afterlife.

- Buddhism teaches that one must follow the Noble Eight-fold Path.
- Islam teaches that one must keep the Five Pillars and lead a righteous life.
- Hinduism teaches that one must adhere to the Four Yogas.
- Sikhism teaches that one must follow his own path and lead a disciplined life.
- Judaism teaches that one must live a moral life according to Torah.
- Mormonism teaches that one must be baptized and obey laws and ordinances.
- Jehovah's Witnesses teach that one must serve and obey Jehovah.
- Roman Catholicism teaches that one must keep the Seven Sacraments.
- Legalistic Protestantism teaches that one must submit to God and obey the Bible.
- Liberal Protestantism teaches that one must do good to others.

While every other religion says "Do," Christianity says "Done!" Grace is God doing everything necessary for our salvation so that we don't have to do anything to be saved. It has been DONE by Christ's death on the cross and His resurrection. We can do nothing to add to that!

## CAN GOOD WORKS PROVE SALVATION?

Some who would agree that we are saved through faith alone and not by works nevertheless teach that works are necessary to prove that salvation is genuine. Instead of frontloading the gospel with works, they backload it. One popular saying is, "We are saved by faith alone, but the faith that saves is never alone." While this may sound good at first, on closer examination it is a nonsensical and contradictory statement, because it says faith must be alone but never alone!

There is every reason to expect that those who have believed in Jesus Christ as Savior and are consequently born into God's family will experience a changed life to some degree. Some want to see this changed life—sometimes called "fruit" or evidence—as proof that a person is saved. But if fruit proves salvation, then the converse is true—if there is no fruit or good works, then there is no salvation. In this view, good works would prove or disprove one's eternal salvation.

Some biblical passages are even used to contend that works can prove or disprove one's eternal salvation. Probably the most common are James 2:14–26; John 15:6; and Matthew 7:15–20.

But James is writing to Christians about the usefulness of their faith, not its genuineness. (We'll look more at that passage later.) Likewise in John 15:6 Jesus is talking about fruitless believers and compares them to branches that are burned—in other words, of not much use. Matthew 7:15–20 warns against false prophets—not believers in general—who can be evaluated on the basis of their evil deeds or heretical teaching—not on an absence of works in general.

There is no passage of Scripture that claims works can prove salvation. In fact, there are many problems with trying to use works to prove salvation—or the lack of works to disprove salvation. Consider the following facts.

*Good works can characterize non-Christians.* Works in and of themselves cannot prove that anyone is eternally saved. Those who have not believed in Christ will often do good things. Good deeds are, in fact, essential to most non-Christian religions. Sometimes the outward morality of non-Christians exceeds that of established Christians.

*Good works can be hard to define.* Though we might define a good work as something done by a Christian through the Spirit and for the Lord, how can we always know when that's true? It's hard to imagine even a single day when a Christian (or non-Christian, for that matter) would not do *something* good, such as provide for a family or hold a door open for someone. How can we know when such things are done through the Spirit and for the Lord, especially if they can be done by non-Christians?

*Good works are relative.* While a person's behavior may seem improper, it could actually demonstrate progress in that person's Christian growth. A man slips with a curse word that startles other believers, but those believers don't know that before his conversion curse words flowed freely. The amount of fruit must be considered in the context of one's total past life, a difficult thing to do. Further, good works could be overlooked in a person's life if an obvious sin draws attention.

*Good works can be passive in nature.* The fruit of salvation is not always what we do, but often what we do not do. As a Christian, one may no longer get drunk or may refrain from yelling at an inconsiderate motorist. This fruit of the Spirit—self-control—may not be detected by others because of its passive nature.

*Good works can be unseen.* In Matthew 6:1–6 Jesus told his followers to give and pray in secret rather than publicly. A person who never prays in a group may breathe a prayer while driving, and no one will ever know. Another may not attend church, but give regularly to a Christian charity. These are works that go unobserved by others.

*Good works can be deceptive.* Since we cannot know a person's motives, a seeming good work could be done for the wrong reason. A woman might give money to a church to impress others. A man might volunteer to work with church children only to wait for an opportunity to abuse them sexually. These are not actually good works at all! Motives are difficult to discern, even for the doer, but God knows each person's heart.[3]

*Good works can be inconsistent.* The Bible allows the possibility of believers who begin well but fall away from their walk with the Lord or fall into sin.[4] If a Christian man or woman shows evidence of a changed life but later falls away, at what point in his or her life do we examine that person to prove or disprove his or her salvation? If there can be lapses in good works, how long does the lapse continue before one is judged as never saved?

Nowhere does the Bible teach that fruit or good works can prove one's eternal salvation. Since the fruit of good works is not easily discerned or quantified, it cannot be reliable proof of salvation. The subjective nature of measuring one's fruit creates the impossibility of knowing objectively whether one is saved. The amount of fruit necessary to please one Christian "fruit inspector" may not please the next "fruit inspector." While good works can be corroborating evidence for one's faith in Christ, they are not sufficient to prove or disprove it. Only faith in God's promise of eternal life through Jesus Christ guarantees and proves our salvation.

## BUT ISN'T FAITH WITHOUT WORKS DEAD?

Absolutely faith without works is dead—James 2:17 says so. But what does that mean? The interpretation of James 2:14–26 has long been controversial and remains so today. Does this passage teach that those who profess faith but have no works are not really saved? Wouldn't this contradict what we've seen in Romans 3–4 or Ephesians 2:8–9 about salvation through faith alone and not by works?

In interpreting this passage we must begin with some important observations. First, there is every indication that the readers were Christians. They were born from above (James 1:18), possessed faith in Christ (2:1), and are called "brethren" (1:2, 19; 2:1, 14; 3:1; 4:11; 5:7, 10, 12, 19). So it would seem contradictory for James to tell some of them that they were not really saved.

Second, the context is bracketed by the theme of judgment (2:13; 3:1). The only judgment that Christians face is the Judgment Seat of Christ. This is not a judgment to see if a person should go to heaven or hell. It is a judgment based on the believer's works or lack of works for the sake of rewards or penalty.[5]

Third, the salvation in mind is not salvation from hell. The word *save* used here is often used of those who are delivered from some undesirable fate.[6] James uses this word in 1:21; 5:15; and 5:20 for a *Christian's* deliverance from some undesirable fate. So he could not be referring to eternal salvation. It is used in 2:14–26 to refer to a Christian delivered from an undesirable fate at the Judgment Seat of Christ such as having his works burned and losing his reward.[7] The profit James speaks of is not salvation, but advantages accrued in this life and the next.

So James is not concerned with the *reality* of his readers' faith, but with the *quality* (compare 1:3, 6; 2:1; 5:15) and *usefulness* (compare 1:12, 26; 2:14, 16, 20) of their faith. James is not saying faith will manifest itself in works, but that without works faith is useless or unprofitable in this life and at the Judgment Seat of Christ. James' main concern is that his readers become "doers of the word"

(1:22), which is the same as being a "doer of the work," because they will be blessed in what they do (1:25). Faith that perseveres in trials, for example, earns a reward from God (1:3–12); faith that is merciful to others receives God's mercy at the Judgment Seat of Christ (2:8–13). But faith that does not work is useless toward these blessings and useless in helping others.[8] The word *dead* should be understood as useless or unprofitable rather than nonexistent.

In 2:19 the faith of demons also shows the uselessness of faith without works. The demons' faith could not save them anyway, because it is only a faith in monotheism (the belief that there is only one God), not in Jesus Christ. James' point in mentioning demons' belief is to argue that they only tremble, and that because they only tremble they do no good works to alleviate a fearful judgment, thus their faith is useless to them.

When James speaks of being "justified by works" (2:21, 24, 25), he is not speaking of the imputed justification that saves us eternally, as Paul uses the term.[9] This would be a contradiction in the Bible. James is speaking of a vindication before other people. Paul even recognizes this use of the word *justify* in Romans 4:2 when he speaks of Abraham's vindication before men. There are two kinds of justification in the Bible. One concerns practical righteousness that vindicates us before people. The other concerns judicial righteousness that vindicates us before God. James obviously uses the practical sense because Abraham was judicially justified in Genesis 15:6 (James 2:23) before he offered Isaac to God in Genesis 22 (2:21). His vindication by others is seen when they call him "the friend of God" (2:23). Thus Abraham's faith was "made perfect" or mature by this demonstration of his faith (2:22).

In 2:26, James is not saying that faith must result in works, but that works make faith come alive, or useful, just as the spirit makes the body useful. The issue is not whether faith exists in a person but how faith becomes profitable or useful to a Christian.

This passage in James, then, is written to Christians to encourage them to do good works, which will make their faith mature and profitable to them and to others. There is no contradiction between James and Paul. When Paul speaks of justification through faith alone, he is speaking of judicial righteousness before God. When James speaks of justification by faith that works, he is speaking of a practical righteousness displayed before other people. In Romans 3–5, Paul is discussing how to obtain a new life in Christ. In James 2:14–26, James is discussing how to make that new life profitable. If this passage is taken to mean that one must demonstrate a *real* salvation through works, then works unavoidably become necessary for salvation—a contradiction of salvation by grace. Further, there is no mention of criteria for exactly what kind or how much work it takes to verify salvation, opening the door to subjectivism and undermining the objective basis of assurance—the promise of God's Word that all who believe in Christ's work will be saved.

## BUT WHAT ABOUT UNCLE JOE?

Everyone knows a man or woman who calls himself or herself a Christian, but doesn't act like one. Christians struggle with how to think about these folks who do not show the works or lifestyle we think they should. Here are some possibilities that might explain these folks.

*They lost their salvation.* We reject this one quickly because of the clear teaching that eternal salvation is eternal and secure.[10] For those who profess to be born-again Christians but fall short of the expected Christian lifestyle, other options explain their behavior more biblically from a grace perspective.

*They were never truly saved.* Perhaps they never understood the facts of the gospel message about the work of Christ on the cross on their behalf. Or perhaps they did not understand the response of faith required of them. They may have made some kind of "decision" or prayed a prayer, but it was based on either false information, peer pressure, or an emotional impulse instead of biblical grounds. They have not believed in the person and work of Jesus Christ alone for eternal life.

*They are Christians who have yet to mature in their Christian walk.* One would expect new Christians to experience a period of growth—out of old habits and worldly tendencies and into a new lifestyle. The length of this growth period may vary, but it is expected that a discernible level of Christian maturity should develop.

*They are Christians who are struggling with sin.* Some Christians because of their past habits, addictions, or personality struggle with the enticements of specific sins, and they sometimes fail. These people with poor behavior may have been Christians for a long time and even seen some growth and change in other areas of their lives. A besetting sin, however, has enslaved them before salvation, perhaps from youth. They find it difficult to break the powerful hold it has on some area of their lives. This could be true of those who were addicted to alcohol, for example, or drugs, or sex.

*They are "backslidden" Christians.* These are true believers who have chosen to live in a worldly way. Some might deny this possibility if the person remains in sin very long. Still, most admit that Christians can make sinful choices and live self-centered lives.

The answer for any of these categories of people lies in the grace of God. They must understand the gospel of grace, grow in it, avail themselves of the Holy Spirit's power given to them, or repent and find the grace of God's forgiveness and restoration.

In the end, only God, and perhaps the people in question, knows for sure whether they who call themselves Christians but don't act like it are truly saved. Works are not a reliable measure. All we can really do is make sure they understand the gospel and the grace of God it represents, and exhort or instruct them in righteousness. If they are true believers, they will have to give an account at the Judgment Seat of Christ for how they lived their lives.

Good works are not at all required to experience God's saving grace, but good works are a natural result of that grace. They are essential to a healthy Christian experience. They make our faith in Jesus Christ useful to others and useful in our final accounting to

God for how we used our lives. But we must be careful in thinking we can easily determine or measure those works in another person's life. That is best left up to God. As we grow in our appreciation of God's grace and as we teach the greatness of His grace, we and others will grow in good works. As believers, we should live godly lives and devote ourselves to good works. But as we will see later, we cannot do that in our own power.

## REVIEW QUESTIONS

1. Explain the difference between the role of good works in salvation and in the Christian life.
2. Why can't good works prove that someone is saved?
3. How would you respond to someone who claims that James 2:14–26 shows that works are necessary to prove our salvation?
4. How can you explain the behavior of someone who claims to be a Christian but does not live like one?

CHAPTER

# A New Accountability

A s mentioned previously, some people think that an emphasis on God's grace will produce an irresponsible lifestyle in believers, an abuse of that grace. "Oh, you have your ticket to heaven," they say, "so you think you can do whatever you want."

But that is not at all a proper understanding of what grace does or the Bible teaches. Consider what Titus 2:11–12 says: "For the grace of God that brings salvation has appeared to all men, teaching us that, denying ungodliness and worldly lusts, we should live soberly, righteously, and godly in the present age."

Grace doesn't teach irresponsibility; it teaches we should be responsible with the grace we have received. The word used in the above passage for *teaching* means "training." It is the word from which we get our English word *pedagogy*, the training of children.

As God's children, we are trained in the negative sense to deny ungodliness and in the positive sense to pursue godliness.

If that is the purpose of grace, then we will be held accountable before God for how we respond to His grace. There are rewards and consequences for the choices we make and the conduct we pursue. God does not let His children run wild. He has positive and negative motivations to influence our conduct.

## WE MUST GIVE AN ACCOUNT

In the New Testament we have the fullest revelation about a time and event where we will have to stand before God to give an account for how we lived. This event is called the Judgment Seat of Christ, sometimes referred to by its Greek designation, the *Bema*. Consider this reference to the *Bema* in Romans 14:10–12:

> But why do you judge your brother? Or why do you show contempt for your brother? For we shall all stand before the Judgment Seat of Christ. For it is written:
> "As I live, says the LORD,
> Every knee shall bow to Me,
> And every tongue shall confess to God."
> So then each of us shall give account of himself to God.

The mention of the Judgment Seat of Christ in this passage is to show these Christians, who were judging one another about controversial issues, that they will ultimately be judged by God, not men.

Note the inclusive emphasis—"we shall all" and "every knee . . . every tongue" and "each of us." No one will be exempt. But the "we" and the whole context of Romans shows that Paul and the Roman believers are in view, so this is a judgment for Christians. Also note that it is a judgment of our conduct, not a judgment of our salvation. Our salvation is an issue settled when we were justified once and forever. Our eternal salvation will never be questioned, but our deeds, conduct, and motivations will face God's scrutiny.

The same truth is also stated clearly in 2 Corinthians 5:10: "For we must all appear before the judgment seat of Christ, that each one may receive the things done in the body, according to what he has done, whether good or bad." Again, Christians are the "we." What we do in this life will determine what we receive from God. Both positive and negative consequences are implied. Let us look more closely at the nature of these consequences.

## POSITIVE CONSEQUENCES

Good conduct and motivations will be rewarded accordingly. The Bible mentions many positive rewards. One important passage is 1 Corinthians 3:11–15:

> For no other foundation can anyone lay than that which is laid, which is Jesus Christ. Now if anyone builds on this foundation with gold, silver, precious stones, wood, hay, straw, each one's work will become clear; for the Day will declare it, because it will be

> revealed by fire; and the fire will test each one's work of
> what sort it is. If anyone's work which he has built on
> it endures, he will receive a reward. If anyone's work is
> burned, he will suffer loss; but he himself will be saved,
> yet so as through fire.

Once the foundation is laid—our relationship with Jesus Christ established through faith—we must build on it. In the immediate context Paul seems to be addressing those who teach believers, but this truth would certainly apply to all Christians. There is a special "Day," the Day we give account at the Judgment Seat of Christ, when God's judgment, which is symbolized here and frequently in the Bible as fire, will test our works. Some will have their works—represented by gold, silver, and precious stones—endure the flames; others will have their works—wood, hay, and straw—burned up. This passage does not speak of the judgment of our salvation and the fire of hell or purgatory. How do we know? Because it is not the person who burns, but the person's works, symbolized by the combustible materials. The passage teaches that those with good works and those with bad works will be saved in the end, even if it is "as through fire." To extend the imagery—some will enter heaven naked and with their hair smoldering!

Apparently those with bad works looked good to others, but didn't pass God's scrutiny. It implies that they had good-looking works but bad motives. Those whose works endure the flames—the gold, silver, precious stones—"will receive a reward." It does not say what that reward will be. In other passages, Jesus taught that He will bring rewards for our works at His coming, though he didn't explain the exact nature of those rewards either.[1]

Though Jesus' rewards are not well defined, it should be enough for us to know that we will be rewarded and that it will be good. Jesus said that we can lay up "treasures in heaven" (Matt. 6:20). Those could not be material treasures, so how we use our lives and our possessions in this life translates into some kind of heavenly wealth.

Some rewards are spoken of as crowns: the crown of rejoicing (1 Thess. 2:19), the crown of righteousness (2 Tim. 4:8), the crown of life (James 1:12), the crown of glory (1 Peter 5:4). Again, the nature of these crowns is not specifically described. It could be that they are used in the sense "the crown *that is* rejoicing," "the crown *that is* righteousness," and so forth. In other words, our reward is the richest experience of rejoicing in God's presence, of richly experiencing His righteousness, His life, and His glory in our eternal state. It implies that there will be degrees of those experiences based on our faithfulness and works in this life.

Another aspect of positive rewards is reigning with Christ in His coming kingdom. The twelve apostles, who left everything to follow Christ, will be rewarded by their sitting on twelve thrones in the kingdom (Matt. 19:27–28). Rewards for others who prove faithful will include ruling over various amounts of cities in the coming kingdom (Luke 19:12–27; see also Matt. 25:14–23). It will also be a major honor to be commended verbally by our Lord.

If our faith is pure and strong in the midst of trials, we will receive praise, honor, and glory in Christ's presence (1 Peter 1:6–7). If we are faithful to confess Christ before others, then Christ will confess us (give a good testimony) to the Father (Matt. 10:32). Also, as with an earthly master's commendation, we can hear our Lord tell us, "Well done" (Matt. 25:21; Luke 19:17).

This is not an exhaustive list of future rewards. We could look in Hebrews at the reward of sharing in the kingdom or look at the "overcomer" rewards to the seven churches in Revelation 2–3. We could also try to be more specific about the exact nature of these positive rewards. But that is not our purpose here. We want to establish the fact that God will hold us accountable for how we spend our lives and that if we do well we will be rewarded.

Our rewards are not only future; some can be temporal, that is, enjoyed in this life. Jesus came to give us His life—eternal life, which we begin to experience at the moment of faith and into eternity—and also the possibility of experiencing His life "more abundantly" both in the present and in eternity (John 10:10). When the disciple Peter implied that he and the other disciples had left everything to follow Jesus, our Lord told him,

> Assuredly, I say to you, there is no one who has left
> house or brothers or sisters or father or mother or wife
> or children or lands, for My sake and the gospel's,
> who shall not receive a hundredfold now in this
> time—houses and brothers and sisters and mothers

and children and lands, with persecutions—and in
the age to come, eternal life (Mark 10:29–30).

For our sacrificial service to Christ we will be rewarded with the
fullest experience of God's eternal life not only in the future but in
this life as well. If we have to leave our biological family for Christ's
sake, we are blessed even more with a spiritual family. We can also
enjoy more "lands" as our own. For example, because of Jesus Christ
I am writing much of this book from a house in the mountains far
from home, which Christian friends who are as close as my own
family have offered for my free use.

## NEGATIVE CONSEQUENCES

If living our Christian lives well will result in positive rewards,
then the converse is true: living irresponsibly will result in negative
consequences. The most obvious negative consequence will be the
loss of the rewards we could have received. First Corinthians 3:15
speaks of those unworthy works that are burned up, representing
a loss of effort and a loss of potential rewards in eternity. Further,
by implication the same passages that teach we can receive rewards
also teach we can lose them. We can lose treasures in heaven,
crowns, ruling privileges, verbal praise, and the abundant experience of God's life in general. We can also lose the experience of
that abundant life here and now, along with losing the blessing of
multiplied spiritual family and "lands."

Other passages teach that we can experience shame and regret at the Judgment Seat of Christ. Jesus may not give us a good confession or testimony if we fail to confess Him before others. "Therefore whoever confesses Me before men, him I will also confess before My Father who is in heaven. But whoever denies Me before men, him I will also deny before My Father who is in heaven" (Matt. 10:32–33). Nothing in the surrounding context of this passage refers to a denial of our salvation. The denial is of a good commendation by the Son to the Father.

Another passage that speaks of a negative consequence at the *Bema* is 1 John 2:28: "And now, little children, abide in Him, that when He appears, we may have confidence and not be ashamed before Him at His coming." This is obviously a word to Christians to encourage them to stay vitally close to Jesus in their walk lest they be caught off guard by His coming and be ashamed.

Just as positive consequences can be experienced in this life, so can negative ones. We know that sin and irresponsibility will always breed the consequences of guilt. Guilt manifests itself in various ways such as spiritual dryness, depression, lack of joy, even physical ailments. In Psalms 32 and 51 we see these negative effects from David's sin.

While sin may have its natural consequences, God may also actively discipline a sinning believer. We are exhorted in Hebrews 12:5–7 to endure God's chastening as from a heavenly Father:

And you have forgotten the exhortation which speaks to you as to sons:

> My son, do not despise the chastening of the LORD,
> Nor be discouraged when you are rebuked by Him;
> For whom the LORD loves He chastens,
> And scourges every son whom He receives.
> If you endure chastening, God deals with you as
>    with sons; for what son is there whom a father
>    does not chasten?

Again, this passage shows that God does not let His children run wild. He is loving enough to correct us with His discipline.

The New Testament shows various ways God disciplines believers. He can do it through leaders in the church who confront a man or woman who sins and may have to dis-fellowship that person if he or she does not repent (Matt. 18:15–17; 1 Cor. 5:1–5). Sometimes God doesn't wait for the church to initiate procedures but takes disciplinary action directly. This seems to be true in the case of Ananias and Sapphira, who dropped dead when they lied (Acts 5:1–11), and the abusers of the Lord's Supper who became ill and died (1 Cor. 11:30).[2] There is sin that leads to physical death (James 5:20; 1 John 5:16).

The negative consequences for sinful and irresponsible Christians can be severe, but they are a necessary corollary to the experience of His grace. Negative consequences discourage us from abusing His grace and show us that God loves us enough not to give up on us, but chastens us so as to bring us to repentance and a deeper experience of His grace. Hebrews 12:11 talks about the desirable results of

God's discipline: "Now no chastening seems to be joyful for the present, but painful; nevertheless, afterward it yields the peaceable fruit of righteousness to those who have been trained by it."

One thing is clear from looking at the negative consequences brought on by sin: when we sin, we lose something, but not our salvation. God's grace is great enough to cover our sins, but not to excuse them.

## THE IMPORTANCE OF REWARDS

Though Jesus and the other New Testament authors speak of rewards and use them as a motivation to faithful Christian conduct, it is sad that we do not often hear rewards taught to Christians. Some Christians do not have a theological category for rewards. In other words, they interpret the rewards and discipline passages as the reward of getting into heaven or the punishment of going to hell. This view often distorts the gospel by making our behavior essential for our salvation, contrary to the free gift of grace. When rewards passages are wrongly interpreted as salvation passages, the unavoidable motivation for doing good works is to validate one's salvation and escape hell. Fear can easily become the motive for good works, but fear of hell can never motivate the believer who is eternally secure. Fear of hell should motivate only the unbeliever. The believer can fear only loss of rewards or fear God's temporal discipline. But even then fear is only one of several other motives for godly living.

Some Christians do believe in rewards, but do not like to teach about them because they think it appeals to a mercenary motive, that is, they think it is not right to do good in order to earn a reward. We know that rewards are not the only, or necessarily the best, motivation for godly living. Love, gratitude, and duty are some of the highest motivations for serving God in this life. But there is nothing wrong with the encouragement and consolation that rewards bring. Since rewards are decreed and designed by God, they shouldn't be considered inferior or scorned in contempt. Every Christian should be taught about rewards.

Think about it this way: if rewards increase our participation in God's glory, or give us a greater capacity to experience God's glory, then our rewards also enable us to give Him more glory. In Revelation 4:10 the twenty-four elders cast their crowns before Christ's throne. Whoever these elders represent, the crowns that they wear certainly symbolize reward, honor, and glory given to them for some reason. They are then able to use that honor to glorify God by offering Him their crowns. In other words, they honor God more by having crowns than if they didn't. The rewards we receive will better enable us to bring Him more glory.

God initiates rewards because He is pleased to do so. So who are we to deny God pleasure? He delights to bless His children with good things. It is a common and commendable human urge to express appreciation for or reward good behavior in our own children. Would we expect less from our heavenly Father?

When we say that grace is unconditional and free, we do not promote irresponsible living or sin. There are consequences to sin that can stretch from this life into the next life, just as there are consequences for our good conduct and faithfulness. We are held accountable for how we choose to live our lives and are recompensed accordingly. These consequences, whether positive or negative, are in harmony with God's grace and justice.

## REVIEW QUESTIONS

1. Why does every Christian need to know about the Judgment Seat of Christ?

2. What are some positive rewards for how we live as Christians? Negative consequences?

3. How can misunderstanding the Bible's teaching on rewards confuse the gospel of grace? Can you give an example?

4. How can rewards be used as a motivation for proper Christian living?

CHAPTER

# A NEW LIFE

Grace has given us the gift of salvation, which we received through faith. There is only one thing better than receiving a free gift—enjoying it! Grace opens up new experiences in a relationship with God that were not possible before we were saved.

## A NEW RESOURCE

The grace that saves us leads us into an even greater experience of grace. "Therefore, having been justified by faith, we have peace with God through our Lord Jesus Christ, through whom also we have access by faith into this grace in which we stand, and rejoice in the hope of the glory of God" (Rom. 5:1–2). The peace of God mentioned here does not refer to an internal peace of heart, but refers to the removal of all enmity between us and God. God's anger at our sin has been removed. We have a new relationship with him as believers, a peaceful one. This new relationship made possible by Christ also gives us access to more grace. This grace is God's provision for whatever is needed to live the Christian life until we are finally glorified with Christ in eternity.

Faith gives us access to the benefits of grace in the new life. We trust God to meet our needs as He promises:

> And my God shall supply all your need according to His riches in glory by Christ Jesus. (Philippians 4:19)

> Let us therefore come boldly to the throne of grace, that we may obtain mercy and find grace to help in time of need. (Hebrews 4:16)

Everything we need to live for Jesus Christ and to serve Him is by His grace and sufficiency. The apostle Paul experienced that in his life and ministry: "And we have such trust through Christ toward God. Not that we are sufficient of ourselves to think of anything as being from ourselves, but our sufficiency is from God" (2 Cor. 3:4–5).

When Paul was suffering a severe trial, Jesus told him, "My grace is sufficient for you, for My strength is made perfect in weakness" (2 Cor. 12:9).

The new life must be lived by faith in God's power and provision. Faith allows Jesus to live His life through us. In Galatians 2:20 Paul expresses his reliance on Jesus Christ's life in him: "I have been crucified with Christ; it is no longer I who live, but Christ lives in me; and the life which I now live in the flesh I live by faith in the Son of God, who loved me and gave Himself for me." The Christian life is a life of faith. But we cannot live it on our own. We walk by faith in Jesus Christ who lives in us.

Just as grace was necessary for our justification, so also grace is necessary for our sanctification. Sanctification is the progressive ongoing aspect of our Christian growth. It literally means "to be set aside" to God, in other words, to become more like Him. In sanctification, grace provides us with a new access, a new identity, a new power, and a new motivation to be more like Jesus Christ.

It is important to see the distinction between justification and sanctification. There is only one condition for justification—belief in Christ as Savior. But sanctification involves belief in Christ as our new Master, whom we must serve in obedience and works. Works do not determine our justification, but they are indispensable to our sanctification. Justification happens the moment we believe, but sanctification happens over our lifetimes. Justification is receiving God's life; sanctification is living it.

## A NEW IDENTITY

A lot happened when we were saved, or justified: we were born into God's family; we were transferred from death (separation from God) into life (union with God); we received God's life; we were adopted as children of God.[1] We have a new identity in Christ.

A central passage about our new identity is Romans 6. In this chapter Paul answers the objections that grace might encourage us to sin. He argues that it does not; we have a new identity because we are joined to Jesus Christ.

> Or do you not know that as many of us as were baptized into Christ Jesus were baptized into His death? Therefore we were buried with Him through baptism into death, that just as Christ was raised from the dead by the glory of the Father, even so we also should walk in newness of life. For we have been united together in the likeness of His death, certainly we also shall be in the likeness of His resurrection. (Romans 6:3–5)

The baptism mentioned in this passage is not water baptism. A physical act could never accomplish a spiritual reality. To baptize means literally to immerse. Paul is describing what happens when we believe in Christ as our Savior. We are immersed or placed into the spiritual body of Jesus Christ. The means by which God does this is His Holy Spirit: "For by one Spirit we were all baptized into one body—whether Jews or Greeks, whether slaves or free—and have all been made to drink into one Spirit" (1 Cor. 12:13).

Every person who believes is baptized by the Holy Spirit into the body of Christ. This baptism unites us with Christ so that just as He died to sin, so have we. "Knowing this, that our old man was crucified with Him, that the body of sin might be done away with, that we should no longer be slaves of sin. For he who has died has been freed from sin" (Rom. 6:6–7).

The crucifixion of our "old man" or the "body of sin," which is "done away with," refers to the overthrow of sin's power in us, in our bodies. Though we are saved, we carry with us the effects of our old lives under the power of sin. But now we have a new Master. We are slaves of Christ, therefore, we are free from the old master, sin. It is important to understand that our sin nature is not destroyed or annihilated; it is overpowered. When a jet plane takes off it does not destroy the law of gravity; it overpowers it with the law of aerodynamics.

As slaves to a new Master, Jesus, we no longer have to answer to the demands made by our old master, sin. If, for example, a man or woman moves to the United States and becomes a citizen, that person no longer has to live under the laws of his or her old country. Before we were saved we had no power to overcome sin. We were like a car with only a reverse gear. But in our new lives, we are like a car with forward gears; we have the ability, through Christ, to live for God.

It is also important to realize that we are united with Christ not only in His death, but also in His resurrection so that we can walk in a new life. "Now if we died with Christ, we believe that we shall also live with Him" (Rom. 6:8). "Likewise you also, reckon yourselves to be dead indeed to sin, but alive to God in Christ Jesus our Lord" (Rom. 6:11).

The word *reckon* means "to come to an informed and conscious conclusion." When we evaluate the facts about Christ's death and resurrection and our union with Him, we must consider ourselves dead to the old master of sin and alive to the new Master, Jesus. We have a new identity as sons of God through Jesus Christ.

The practical implication of this is expressed in Romans 6:12–13:

> Therefore do not let sin reign in your mortal body, that you should obey it in its lusts. And do not present your members as instruments of unrighteousness to sin, but present yourselves to God as being alive from the dead, and your members as instruments of righteousness to God.

Our obedience to our new Master is carried out in how we use our bodies, which includes our minds. If we choose to sin we will experience a sense of separation from God, which is described in Romans 6:23: "For the wages of sin is death." But the same verse tells us that if we willingly offer ourselves to God for His service, we will experience God's righteousness and holiness, or what is called God's eternal life: "but the gift of God is eternal life in Christ Jesus our Lord."[2] For a believer, sin is related to fellowship, not salvation. Sin interrupts the joy of experiencing Jesus' gift of eternal life, the life of God who is in us.

As Christians we must *choose* to live in our new identities as children of God and servants of God. When we do so, we will not return to serve our old master, sin. We will grow in our experience of God's eternal life.

## A NEW POWER

Another key factor about living our new lives is that we cannot do it by our own effort. In Romans 7:14–23 Paul describes his effort to live for God but in his own strength. He says,

> For we know that the law is spiritual, but I am carnal, sold under sin. For what I am doing, I do not understand. For what I will to do, that I do not practice; but what I hate, that I do. If, then, I do what I will not to do, I agree with the law that it is good. But now, it is no longer I who do it, but sin that dwells in me. For I know that in me (that is, in my flesh) nothing good dwells; for to will is present with me, but how to perform what is good I do not find. For the good that I will to do, I do not do; but the evil I will not to do, that I practice. Now if I do what I will not to do, it is no longer I who do it, but sin that dwells in me. I find then a law, that evil is present with me, the one who wills to do good. For I delight in the law of God according to the inward man. But I see another law in my members, warring against the law of my mind, and bringing me into captivity to the law of sin which is in my members.

Perhaps you have felt the same frustration of trying to do what you know is right only to fail and do what you know is wrong.

Paul describes the struggle we have with the sin that remains in us. Though sin no longer has the right to rule over us, it can sometimes exert itself powerfully. Just as a snake with its head cut off is doomed but can still writhe for quite a while afterward, so the rule of death is doomed but its influence can still be felt in our bodies. Paul's struggle with sin was so intense, he cried out, "O wretched man that I am! Who will deliver me from this body of death?" (Rom. 7:24).

In our struggle with sin, how can we have the victory? If we can't do it in our own strength, what power can overcome our sinful urges so that we can obey God and do right? Paul answers this for us in Romans 7:25: "I thank God—through Jesus Christ our Lord! So then, with the mind I myself serve the law of God, but with the flesh the law of sin." To live in victory over sin we must allow the Lord Jesus to live His life through us. His life is God's gracious gift to us, the gift of eternal life.

The way that Jesus lives in us is through His Holy Spirit, who indwells us. We must fix our minds on the Spirit so that the Spirit can control our minds, because our minds control our bodies. The power of the Holy Spirit exerted over our minds will give us victory over sin.

Romans 8:1–6 contrasts the life controlled by the flesh with the life controlled by the Spirit:

> There is therefore now no condemnation to those
> who are in Christ Jesus, who do not walk according

to the flesh, but according to the Spirit. For the law
of the Spirit of life in Christ Jesus has made me free
from the law of sin and death. For what the law
could not do in that it was weak through the flesh,
God did by sending His own Son in the likeness of
sinful flesh, on account of sin: He condemned sin in
the flesh, that the righteous requirement of the law
might be fulfilled in us who do not walk according
to the flesh but according to the Spirit. For those
who live according to the flesh set their minds on the
things of the flesh, but those who live according to
the Spirit, the things of the Spirit. For to be carnally
minded is death, but to be spiritually minded is life
and peace.

We cannot live the Christian life by the *flesh*, which means
by our own efforts. It is not a matter of trying harder. We need
a supernatural power assist—the Holy Spirit, God's gift to us.
When we allow the Spirit to control our minds, we will obey
God and live righteously. The power of the Spirit overpowers the
effects of sin and death in us. A caterpillar is confined to the
earth by the law of gravity until it grows wings. Then it can fly
above the earth because the law of aerodynamics gives it a new
power over gravity. When God's Spirit is allowed to control our
minds, we are able to do what is right. We will enjoy His life as
He lives through us.

## A NEW MOTIVATION

But why do we want to live to please God? Why would we feel the frustration that Paul expressed about doing the wrong things when we know the right? Before we came to know Christ, life was likely motivated by fear to some degree—a constant nagging fear that we will be judged and condemned for our sin, the feeling that we had not done enough to please God. But in our new life in Christ, we are no longer in bondage to fear because we are now children of God. As children of a loving and gracious heavenly Father, we want to please Him.

Romans 12:1 is a pivotal passage in the epistle and crucial in our discussion of a new motivation. Paul says, "I beseech you therefore, brethren, by the mercies of God, that you present your bodies a living sacrifice, holy, acceptable to God, which is your reasonable service." One clue that this passage is pivotal is the word *therefore.* Paul is drawing a conclusion from his previous discussion in chapters 1–11. In short, those chapters demonstrate God's grace to us, from our justification through our sanctification, our eternal security, and our divine selection.

What is the only "reasonable" response to the overwhelming and tenacious grace of God revealed to us in Jesus Christ? It is to surrender ourselves to Him as a sacrifice, a living sacrifice useful to God. Our bodies contain all of us—our minds, our wills, and our members that can serve God.

But again, why would we do this? It is not required of us to keep our salvation. When we realize how God's grace has blessed us, we might want to do it out of gratitude. We might also do it out of love because we realize He loved us first (1 John 4:19). Love begets love. We might surrender ourselves to His service because we realize that what we do has eternal significance with consequences that stretch into eternity. These are all new motivations for us who once lived in fear and uncertainty.

"The gift of God is eternal life in Christ Jesus our Lord" (Rom. 6:23). What profound words! Because of God's gift we have a new life in which we have access to all the resources of God to live a godly life. We also have a new identity in Jesus Christ. He is our new Master. By God's grace we have the Holy Spirit to give us power over sin. And because of God's grace we have new motivations to serve Him: love, gratitude, and eternal significance. Truly His grace is sufficient!

## REVIEW QUESTIONS

1. Explain how salvation by grace can lead us to a greater experience of grace.

2. In what ways can Christians continue to experience God's grace?

3. What are some implications of having a new identity?

4. What should be the prevailing motivation for living a godly life?

# A NEW COMMITMENT

As we enjoy a new life in Christ, we can also enjoy a new purpose. When we are motivated to serve God out of love and gratitude for His grace, we look for the best way to do that. When Jesus preached the gospel and people believed, He then challenged those believers to become disciples. To become a disciple of Jesus Christ is, in short, to offer yourself as a "living sacrifice" to God. It is a way of life open to anyone who has believed in Christ as Savior and now wants to serve Him as Lord. It is a possibility provided by grace.

## THE MEANING OF DISCIPLESHIP

The word *disciple* comes from the word *to learn*. So a disciple is a learner, a pupil, or an apprentice. Sometimes in the Gospels discipleship is referred to as "following" Jesus Christ. In Jesus' time a rabbi (teacher) would gather around himself those who wanted to learn from him and become like him. These pupils would follow closely and live with their master to learn all they could. Their lives were devoted to becoming like their master. In Matthew 10:25 Jesus said, "It is enough for a disciple that he be like his teacher, and a servant like his master."

Though Jesus is no longer with us physically, we can still be His disciples if we commit to learn from Him so that we can become like Him. That commitment should be our response to the grace we realized in salvation. In Matthew 11:28–30 Jesus gives an invitation to salvation and an invitation to discipleship: "Come unto Me, all you who labor and are heavy laden, and I will give you rest. Take my yoke upon you and learn from Me, for I am gentle and lowly in heart, and you will find rest for your souls. For My yoke is easy and My burden is light."

The call to salvation is in the invitation to "Come" to Jesus Christ. Those who come receive "rest" in God's righteousness instead of having to struggle for their own. Jesus offers His righteousness as a free gift to all who receive it through faith. That refers to our justification. The call to discipleship, however, is seen in the invitation "Take My yoke . . . and learn from Me." The imagery of a yoke that binds an ox to a plow is a picture of discipline and obligation. Sometimes a younger animal was trained by yoking it to an older, stronger animal. Jesus invites us to be yoked to Him. He is inviting submission to His teaching and authority. When we accept His invitation to be a disciple, we find further rest for our souls. The word "souls" can also be translated "lives." The life of a disciple is a life of peace and rest as we learn from Christ and follow His will. That is also called our sanctification.

Following Jesus is not necessarily easy, but since we are yoked to Christ, He is the stronger one. God's grace is sufficient to help us make and keep our commitments to Him. Living in partnership with Jesus is always the easiest way to live, because we have the joy of serving Him and the resources of the Spirit's power to do His will.

## THE DISTINCTIONS OF DISCIPLESHIP

It should now be apparent that discipleship is distinct from one's initial salvation; disciples are made not born. If salvation is free—by grace through faith—but discipleship is costly, then salvation must be distinct from discipleship. This chart should help show the distinctions between salvation and discipleship:

| SALVATION | DISCIPLESHIP |
|---|---|
| Free gift | Costly |
| Received through faith | Requires commitment and obedience |
| Does not involve our works | Involves our works |
| Instant justification | Lifelong sanctification |
| Jesus paid the price | The Christian pays the price |
| Coming to Jesus as Savior | Following Jesus as Lord |
| Believe the gospel | Obey the commands |
| "A" truth | "B" truth |

This distinction is crucial to keeping the gospel of salvation clear, because if we confuse the distinctives of discipleship with the gift of salvation, grace will no longer be free. Salvation would cost us all of the commitments and sacrifices required to be a disciple.

A helpful way to keep salvation distinct from discipleship is to think of salvation as "A" truth and discipleship as "B" truth. Just as "A" comes before "B," salvation comes before discipleship. So "A" truth includes all the things we read in the Bible about our need for salvation, the condition for our salvation, the consequences of heaven and hell, and the consequences of eternal life or death. On the other hand, "B" truth includes all the commands and promises to the Christian after salvation, or in our sanctification. Things like discipleship, commitments, rewards, discipline, growth, and service are all "B" truth.

Keeping salvation and discipleship distinct will help you appreciate each of them more. It will also help you interpret many of the discipleship passages in the Bible that people confuse as being about salvation. Salvation is free, but discipleship is costly. Both are a result of the grace of God working in our lives.

## THE COST OF DISCIPLESHIP

So what does it cost to become a disciple? In one sense, it costs everything. But Jesus made some specific demands for Christians who wanted to follow Him as disciples. When we examine the contexts of these demands, we see that consistently they are given to those who had already believed and even those who were already called disciples. The unbeliever would not comprehend these demands or be motivated to meet them. Believers have experienced God's grace, which teaches and motivates them to meet the demands. Even those who are already disciples need to be challenged to be more of a disciple, because discipleship is not a static state. As we grow, God constantly makes more demands and requires more commitments of us.

Let us now look at some of the major conditions of discipleship. A very important one concerns the believer's relationship to God through His Word. "Then Jesus said to those Jews who believed in Him, 'If you abide in My word, you are My disciples indeed. And you shall know the truth, and the truth shall make you free'" (John 8:31–32). To *abide* means "to continue in" or "remain in." Use of the word *abide* assumes that because these Christians have believed, have begun in Christ's Word, they must now continue to follow and obey it. They will establish themselves in the truth, and the nature of truth is that it frees us from theological and moral falsehoods that could bring us into bondage to error and sin. To be disciples, we must devote ourselves to knowing and following God's Word, which we have today in the Bible.

Three more conditions of discipleship are stated in Luke 9:23. Jesus said, "If anyone desires to come after Me, let him deny himself, and take up his cross daily, and follow Me."

The first of the conditions in this verse—to deny oneself— means to put God's will before our own, to say *no* to our self-interests and desires in order to say *yes* to God's desires for us. It is a repudiation of our own will and choosing God's will instead. We say *no*, for example, to our desires for selfish ambition, sinful pleasures, or revenge so that we can adopt God's goals for our lives, find our pleasure in Him, and allow God to deal with those who harm us.

To take up the cross is to be willing to suffer hardships because of our identification with Jesus Christ or our desire to do His will. In New Testament times the cross denoted the cruelest form of suffering and death. Disciples are willing to suffer for Jesus, which sometimes means that, even today, we could pay with our lives. To tell someone to take up his cross is like saying, "Bring your own bullet" or "Pack the cyanide." Almost every day we have opportunities to identify with Jesus Christ and do His will in the face of opposition, ridicule, or persecution. Can we follow Jesus in suffering for Him?

The third condition here is to follow Christ. This is an invitation to live with Jesus in the closest possible relationship so that we are doing His will and fulfilling His purpose for our lives. When Jesus invited Peter, Andrew, James, and John to follow Him, He told them He would make them "fishers of men."[1] To follow Jesus' purpose for our lives will at least involve bringing other people to Him. Jesus said His purpose was to preach the gospel and to seek and save the lost.[2] We can fulfill this purpose wherever we are—at work, at leisure, or at home.

Another condition Jesus gave looks very difficult: "If anyone comes to Me and does not hate his father and mother, wife and children, brothers and sisters, yes, and his own life also, he cannot be My disciple" (Luke 14:26). When Jesus says "hate," though, He is using a figure of speech that means "love less than." A disciple must make Jesus the object of supreme love and devotion, even to a greater degree than his own family—even more than his own life! This does not mean that we neglect our loved ones. It will, in fact, result in loving them more. But sometimes serving our family relationships and our own desires will test our loyalty to Jesus. We must put Him first in all of our relationships if we would be His disciples.

In the same passage Jesus also says, "Whoever of you does not forsake all . . . cannot be My disciple" (Luke 14:33). He illustrates this demand with a builder and a king who did not commit the necessary provisions to finish their work. It shows that as believers we must commit whatever possessions are necessary to do what God asks us to do. This is a matter of stewardship, because if God owns everything, we must be willing to manage it faithfully and surrender it to Him when He asks us to.

There are other conditions for discipleship as well. But the ones we have listed all involve a commitment, obedience, or some kind of sacrifice from the Christian. If that is true, then discipleship costs the believer something, maybe everything. Can you see why the conditions for discipleship cannot be conditions for salvation, which is by grace through faith?

## THE PROCESS OF DISCIPLESHIP

Unlike our salvation (or justification), which is an instantaneous event, discipleship is a lifelong process. After seeing the conditions necessary to become a disciple, it's easy to understand why disciples are made not born. Not every Christian is a disciple, though every disciple must be a Christian. Discipleship is like a journey.

Each disciple's journey proceeds at a different pace. There are times of great progress, slower progress, stagnation, and even losing ground. But a Christian is a disciple so long as he or she is committed to Jesus Christ and the journey to become Christlike.

A good example of the journey of discipleship is the life of the apostle Peter. In John's account, Peter met the Lord early in John 1 and had believed in him by John 2:11 and 6:68–69. Yet his life as Jesus' disciple shows times of weak faith and even denial of Jesus. Still, Peter is always considered a disciple. It is interesting that Jesus continually tells Peter to follow, or we see Peter mentioned as following not only in his earlier time with Jesus but also in his denial at Jesus' arrest and after Jesus' resurrection.[3] As I said, there is a sense in which a disciple is always challenged to become more of a disciple.

The fact that Peter is always listed first among the disciples, was usually their spokesman, and was one of the three closest to Jesus shows that God may have intended us to view him as a picture of the discipleship journey. Peter is someone we can identify with. He illustrates both the demands of discipleship and the grace that God provides to follow Him even after failure. Like Peter, we should expect our journey to be full of twists and turns, but ultimately headed in the right direction—toward Christ.

## THE PURPOSE OF DISCIPLESHIP

A disciple's life is a life of purpose. To follow Jesus includes "fishing" for people so they can believe and follow Him too. Jesus issued a final command before leaving earth and ascending into heaven:

> And Jesus came and spoke to them, saying, "All au-
> thority has been given to Me in heaven and on earth.
> Go therefore and make disciples of all the nations,
> baptizing them in the name of the Father and of the
> Son and of the Holy Spirit, teaching them to observe
> all things that I have commanded you; and lo, I am
> with you always, even to the end of the age." Amen.
> (Matthew 28:18–20)

Jesus left us with a strategy for purposeful and effective ministry. We are to multiply ourselves in the lives of other people by
making disciples. The way this imperative is written in the original
language shows that "make disciples" is the main command. The
subordinate actions in the command explain *how* we make disciples: by going out to evangelize, by baptizing believers into the
fellowship of Christ's church, and by teaching those believers so
they can be disciples themselves.

As we obediently follow Jesus and all that He taught us, we
show that we love God and we will grow closer to Him (John
14:21). Because we love God and follow Christ we will also love
and serve others (John 13:35). There is no higher purpose in life
than to love and serve God and others.

The first step in your lifelong journey of purpose is, of course,
to grow as a disciple yourself. We previously discussed the greatest resource for growth—God's Spirit in us—but we have other
resources that can also help. First of all is the church through its

teaching, fellowship, worship, and opportunities for ministry. There is also some good literature you can use, although I must caution you that not all of it is consistent in its view of the gospel, grace, and what it means to be a disciple. I have written a workbook specifically to help people get grounded in grace, grow as a disciple, and help them make disciples of others.[4] You can also find a more mature Christian or a group of mature Christians and spend time with them, studying the Bible and learning to apply it to life. The important thing is to get started and grow so that you can pass it on to others.

To follow Jesus as a disciple is a commitment every believer should make. To fully appreciate God's gift of grace is to grow in it and in our relationship to the God of all grace. It is unfortunate that many times the commitments of discipleship are misunderstood as commitments needed for salvation. This undermines the grace of God and the work that Jesus Christ has done for us. This interpretation not only makes assurance of salvation impossible, it also removes the foundation for a life of joy and freedom, which comes from growing in grace. The possibility of discipleship is a gift of grace. The ability to keep the commitments of discipleship is also ultimately by God's grace as we cooperate with the Holy Spirit in us and abide in His Word.

## REVIEW QUESTIONS

1. What should be the goal of a disciple?

2. How would you distinguish between salvation and discipleship and why is that important?

3. Explain the statement "Disciples are made not born."

4. How do the conditions for discipleship relate to the lifelong journey of discipleship?

CHAPTER

# A NEW FREEDOM

Chan Zhong Bing came to America in the late 1870s to pursue a better life for himself and his family back in China. He was recruited by dishonest agents in China who promised a job and freedom. What he got was virtual slavery to the dirtiest and most dangerous jobs in building the railroads and constant indebtedness to his employer. Somehow Chan was able to break free and make his way to Washington, D.C., where he opened a Chinese restaurant.

Wu Ah Choy arrived in America as a servant girl when she was about eight years old, having been sold to a rich Chinese-American, a fate shared by many girls from poor Chinese families. At the age of thirteen she was sold again to another Chinese-American and soon became pregnant before she knew what pregnant was. That son died, as did the next. Because her master was physically and verbally abusive, Wu, at the age of sixteen broke through a wall to freedom and ran away, leaving her third son with her master. What she did to survive as a non-English speaking Chinese girl in a strange country is a mystery she never revealed, but somehow she eventually met Chan and they married. They had a boy, my father, and named him Robert. His is the only generation between me and slavery.

My grandfather abandoned my grandmother and father and returned to China during the Great Depression. I never knew him or communicated with him. My grandmother remained in Washington, D.C., where one Sunday she attended a church class taught by a Chinese-speaking former missionary. She heard the gospel and believed it. Her journey to freedom was complete. I am an heir of her struggle for social freedom, but now I also enjoy her spiritual freedom through Jesus Christ, and I take neither for granted.

## FULLY FREE

What is freedom worth to you? Some consider personal freedom more precious than possessions or life itself. A country's citizens will fight to the death to remain free. But what about spiritual freedom? What good would political and personal freedom be if we were spiritual slaves to sin, fear of condemnation, or fear of death?

In my observation, spiritual freedom is a rare experience in this world. Billions of people are bound in the darkness of unbelief, fearing both life and death. They live in fear of displeasing their gods and they die in fear of their unknown fate.

The situation with Christians is better, but often not as good as it could be. While Christians should live confidently in hope, too many live fearfully, thinking that their God is displeased with them. While they believe that heaven and eternal life should be their future, they are confused and uncertain whether they will be "good enough" to get there or experience it.

No one can have spiritual freedom who has not experienced grace, because grace sets us free. Those who have not experienced the grace of God in salvation are in spiritual darkness and bondage. But those who have been saved can also live in bondage to fear. They have not experienced grace to the fullest.

## GRACE SETS US FREE

Consider what happens the moment we believe in Jesus Christ as our Savior:

- We are free from the penalty of our sins.
- We are free from God's condemnation.
- We are free from the fear of death.
- We are free from the fear of uncertainty about eternity.
- We are free from the guilt that sin brings.

Also consider what happens as we grow in our experience of that same grace:

- We are free from obedience to the power of sin.
- We are free from the demands of the Law for acceptance with God.

- We are free from the power of Satan over us.
- We are free to serve God and others.
- We are free to be all that God made us to be.

When we believe the gospel, we are free because God has delivered us from death, the Devil, error, sin's power, and a host of other bondages. It is unfortunate when those who have been set free live as though they were still in prison.

## FREE TO GROW

The freedom that grace brings is the fertile soil for spiritual growth. Fear causes us to live protectively and anxiously. There's a big difference between the attitude of a slave and that of a son. Romans 8:15 says to believers, "For you did not receive the spirit of bondage again to fear, but you received the Spirit of adoption by whom we cry out, 'Abba, Father.'" The term *Abba* is a respectful and affectionate term for one's father, like *Papa* or *Daddy*. It shows familiarity and family relation. God is now our Father and we are His children. How does a perfect Father treat His children?

Every father knows that newborns will make a mess, that children will stumble and fall, and that part of growing up is making bad choices. As our Father, God does not expect perfection from us. He knows we will stumble and fall and sin. He understands better than we that our growth and sanctification is a process. When we fall, God does not kick us out of the family or cease to be our Father. Like a good father He restores the fellowship that was broken. The certainty of our failures and the possibility of restoration is not an excuse to sin; it is just a reality.

As a good Father, God in His grace has provided the way to restore fellowship when we sin by allowing us to confess our sins and receive His forgiveness and cleansing: "If we confess our sins, He is faithful and just to forgive us our sins and to cleanse us from all unrighteousness" (1 John 1:9). To *confess* means "to say the same thing as" or "to agree with" God that we were wrong. No sin is too great to keep us from fellowship with God if we confess it to Him. He can forgive us and restore fellowship with us because His grace is greater than all our sin (Rom. 5:20).

What this means is that we can live confidently, knowing that our Father loves us and accepts us. We are free to be ourselves and to serve God in our unique way. We should live without fearing that God is waiting for us to mess up so he can destroy us. If we sin, He forgives and restores. Even at our worst times we know that God is for us, not against us. On our worst days, He is with us. He is on our side.

The gospel of grace sets us free. But no one is free in the absolute sense. So how do we exercise our freedom in Christ? If freedom is not controlled, it can be perverted.

## ABUSING FREEDOM WITH LICENSE

One way freedom can be perverted is through license. This is the abuse of grace to serve oneself selfishly and sinfully. It is an unrestrained life that scorns God's commands. Jude 4 warns of "ungodly men, who turn the grace of God into lewdness and deny the only Lord God and our Lord Jesus Christ." There are groups and individuals who teach grace as an excuse to sin.

Christians who fall into license may reason that they can indulge in sin because their eternal salvation cannot be lost, or because they are forgiven already, or at least, they rationalize, "God will forgive me when I sin." This is the immature and uniformed attitude behind the objections we noted in Romans 6:1 and 6:15. There the question is, "Should we sin to experience more grace and because we are not under the Law?" Paul's answer is, *absolutely not!* In Christ, we have died to sin and we are under a new Master, Jesus Christ, whom we should serve. Also we have seen in Romans 6 and in other Scriptures that there are serious negative consequences for sin. In our discussion of eternal security we saw that grace is not a license to sin.

Those who reject all commands are called *antinomians*, which means "against the law," or "opposed to the law." While there may be some who deserve that title, it does not describe what I have said about grace and the Christian life. We believe that grace frees us from the Old Testament Law, because its demands were fully met on our behalf by Jesus Christ. But we realize the New Testament has laws to fulfill.

Under Christ, we have many commands to fulfill, not to earn salvation but to *grow* in our salvation. Though we are not under the Mosaic Law, the New Testament has commands to obey, chief among them is to love God and to love our neighbor, both of which preclude self-serving and sinful behavior. The licentious Christian fails to realize how he or she is despising grace and how such conduct forfeits fellowship with God in this life and forfeits benefits in eternity, and it invites God's disciplinary action.

Simply put, the freedom that grace provides is not freedom to do what we want, but freedom to do what God wants. Such freedom can be abused. That is why Paul was compelled to tell the Galatians believers, "For you, brethren, have been called to liberty; only do not use liberty as an opportunity for the flesh, but through love serve one another" (Gal. 5:13). When we see freedom as an opportunity to serve others and please God, we will not drift into licentiousness.

## RESTRICTING FREEDOM THROUGH LEGALISM

Grace can be perverted not only by license, but it can also be perverted by legalism. Legalism is the abuse of grace that seeks to bring Christians back under either the Mosaic Law or some artificial standard for acceptance with God that has been created by others. The legalist insists on following a list of "dos and don'ts" such as those that seem to be behind the warnings against legalism in Galatians and Colossians.[1]

There's nothing wrong with following biblical "dos and don'ts" if we obey them out of a love for God and a desire to please Him. We become legalistic only if we demand obedience to commands or principles that are not in the Bible or if we obey them in order to exalt ourselves before God and others. Attitude and motive is key.

Christians can easily fall under the legalism of others, which can lead to feelings of false guilt. Those under legalism can, for example, be made to feel that they are not spiritual because of what Bible translation they use, how they dress, what movies they see, what music they listen to, what church meetings they do or do not attend—or any other issue that the Bible does not address directly.

What the legalist fails to realize is that Jesus not only set us free from the Old Testament Law[2] but He also set us free from artificial man-made standards that are not in the Bible. We are accepted by God because we are His children by grace, not by performance. We stand accepted by His grace and are thus secured by His grace until the time when we see Him. Since every believer is accepted on the basis of grace we should accept other believers who differ on issues not clearly defined as right or wrong in the Bible (see the discussion below). Legalists have "fallen from grace" (Gal. 5:4) in that they now rely on their own performance to complete their relationships with God. What they don't understand is that they must always perform perfectly or they are condemned by their own standards, whatever they are.

Those who teach legalism, practice legalism, or find themselves under legalism are generally miserable people. They learn to conform on the outside without genuine change on the inside. They live under the pressure of constantly trying to please an angry God or judgmental people. Depression, burnout, and dropout are often the consequences. If you find yourself under legalism, flee from it as soon as you can!

Only Jesus Christ's perfect performance is acceptable to God, and therefore only Christians who trust in that gracious provision are acceptable to God. The way to please God and live up to the standards of the Law is to love.

## CONTROLLING FREEDOM THROUGH LOVE

The balance between the extremes of license and legalism is love. When we love God and others, we will not live sinfully or under artificial demands. Love is the controlling principle that constrains the proper and godly use of our freedom (Gal. 5:13–14). Our liberty must be exercised in love to avoid the extremes of license and legalism.

| LICENSE | LIBERTY | LEGALISM |
| --- | --- | --- |

### LOVE

When Jesus was asked what was the greatest commandment, He answered, "'You shall love the Lord your God with all your heart, with all your soul, and with all your mind.' This is the first and great commandment. And the second is like it: 'You shall love your neighbor as yourself.' On these two commandments hang all the Law and the Prophets" (Matt. 22:37–40).

Jesus knew that when a man or woman loves God, that person will please Him and will love others. "Love your neighbor" is not a command "second" in importance, but second in the sense that it is inseparable from the first, like the two halves of a pair of scissors or the two legs of a pair of pants. All the moral teaching of the Old Testament Law and prophets as well as the New Testament is fulfilled when we love God and others. Perhaps you can see why someone has said, "Love God with all your heart and do what you please."

Sometimes our freedom can be exercised in a way that hurts others, in other words, in an unloving way. Of course, many sins we might commit could hurt other people, Christian and non-Christian alike. It is difficult to love all people. Referring to Jesus' words in Matthew 5:44, Will Rogers once said, "The Bible says 'Love your enemies,' but why don't you try it out on your friends for a while!"

Christians must learn to exercise their freedom around other Christians who may not agree with them about things not specifically addressed in the Bible. We call these gray areas "questionable practices." Christians can differ, for example, about the use of alcoholic beverages, what movies are appropriate to watch, or what holidays to celebrate and how to celebrate them. There are many controversial issues. One Christian may do one of these activities with a clear conscience and a belief that it is part of the freedom she has under grace in Christ. But another will not do it because he believes it is sin. So how are they to get along?

There are a number of principles that will help us exercise our freedom and allow others to exercise their freedom under grace. Some of these principles come from long discussions about questionable practices like the one found in Romans 14.

- We must accept those who differ in their opinion about questionable practices because God has accepted them (14:1–3).

- We should not judge a believer about questionable practices because we are not that believer's Judge (14:3–4).

- We must honor a believer's convictions about what pleases God (14:5–9).

- We should be more concerned about giving an account to God for our own choices (14:10–12).

- We must never do anything that would lead other Christians to sin (14:13–23).

- We should always put the best interests of others ahead of our own (15:1–7).

Another extended discussion is in 1 Corinthians 8–10. From the conclusion to this discussion we can ask four questions to help determine if a questionable practice is right for us.

1. Does it enslave me or does it edify me? (1 Cor. 6:12; 10:23)
2. Does it cause hurt or does it help the other believer? (1 Cor. 10:24–29)
3. Does it glorify God? (1 Cor. 10:30–31)
4. Does it hurt or does it help my witness to unbelievers? (1 Cor. 10:32–33)

In short, our liberty should always be controlled by love. When Paul wrote the exhortation of Galatians 5:13–14, he was remembering Jesus' words: "For you, brethren, have been called to liberty; only do not use liberty as an opportunity for the flesh, but through love serve one another. For all the law is fulfilled in one word, even in this: 'You shall love your neighbor as yourself.'" Then Paul states that the key to love is walking in the Spirit so that the Holy Spirit controls our lives (Gal. 5:15–26). The first fruit of the Spirit is love (Gal. 5:22).

## FREEDOM WORTH FIGHTING FOR

I hope that as you come to a healthy appreciation of God's magnificent grace and the freedom it provides, you value it worth fighting for. Not in an ungracious combative sense, but that you defend the freeness of grace and its glorious liberty. The Scriptures show us that whenever and wherever Paul preached his gospel of grace, there followed those who would pervert the message and lead people back into bondage. Thus he admonishes the Galatians who were being persuaded by those who opposed God's grace, "Stand fast therefore in the liberty by which Christ has made us free, and do not be entangled again with a yoke of bondage" (Gal. 5:1).

It's easy to get back into the performance system of trying to please God, or to allow others to make us feel guilty with their false standards of spirituality. But to loosely paraphrase Paul, "Don't just *do* something; *stand* there!" Stand firm in grace. Remember that God paid the highest price for your freedom. He gave His only Son, Jesus Christ, "Knowing that you were not redeemed with corruptible things, like silver or gold, . . . but with the precious blood of Christ, as of a lamb without blemish and without spot" (1 Peter 1:18–19).

We should not allow the precious gospel to be polluted with the arrogant attitude that it can be improved by anything we can do. We can add nothing to God's gift of salvation and God's unconditional acceptance. It is *only by grace* and *simply by grace* that we have been saved, can know we are saved, will stay eternally saved, and can live a life pleasing to God. Never surrender your position in grace! "You therefore, my son, be strong in the grace that is in Christ Jesus" (2 Tim. 2:1). Instead, let us continue to strengthen our position. "But grow in the grace and knowledge of our Lord and Savior Jesus Christ. To Him be the glory both now and forever. Amen" (2 Peter 3:18).

## REVIEW QUESTIONS

1. What does grace free us *from*? What does grace free us *to*?
2. What is a biblical attitude toward grace and license?
3. Why is legalism an enemy of grace?
4. How should love control our freedom under grace?

# SHARING THE GIFT

When we encounter the life-changing gift of grace in the gospel, we should naturally want to share it with others. When we share the gospel, we must keep it simple, clear, and absolutely free.[1]

## KEEP IT CLEAR

Once, when I was invited to preach at an evangelistic meeting, the organizing pastor introduced me to a dear woman before the meeting. He had talked with her previously, but remained unsure whether she was saved or not. He left me alone with her, so I asked some "diagnostic" questions to find out for myself. I concluded that she did not really understand the gospel, so I explained it to her as clearly as I could, then led her to place her faith in Christ.

When we returned to the pastor to tell him the good news, she instead pointed her finger in his face and in an accusing voice rebuked him, "Why didn't you explain it clearly to me? You never made it clear!" It is hard to say who was more embarrassed—I or the pastor who had just graduated from seminary a "Master of Theology"! Academic credentials are no guarantee of clarity in communication.

In Colossians 4:4 Paul asks for prayer to make his gospel-telling "*manifest*, as I ought to speak" (emphasis added). The New American Standard Version and the New International Version prefer the word *clear* or *clearly*. One commentator translates this verse this way: "that I may publish it openly in the words which I ought to speak." Paul understood it was easy to garble the gospel. He wanted to word it clearly. The word he used has the idea of "to make visible" and is from a word that means "to manifest" or "to light up." The job of the gospel-teller is to shed light on the message, or make it clear, not to obscure it.

God can save more people with a clear message than with a cloudy one. A clear presentation of the gospel is not only more powerful, it also gets people off to a well-grounded start in their Christian walk. We will look at several elements that make for a clear gospel witness.

## A CLEAR CONTENT

What does a person have to believe in to be saved? I have heard everything from "Believe in God" and "the Ten Commandments" (or "the Sermon on the Mount") to "Just believe that Jesus loves you." What is the content of the gospel and how can we articulate it clearly?

The gospel's content is laid out no more clearly than by Paul in

1 Corinthians 15. Paul reminds the Corinthians about the gospel that he preached, that they received, and by which they were saved (15:1–2). The message was the one Paul received personally from God (15:3; compare Gal. 1:1–12).

In 1 Corinthians 15:3–5 we find two great propositions of the gospel and their supporting evidence. We could diagram the verses like this:

| | |
|---|---|
| Christ died for our sins | 1) First proposition |
|     according to the Scriptures |   1a) Scriptural proof |
|     and was buried |   1b) Physical proof |
| He arose | 2) Second proposition |
|     according to the Scriptures |   2a) Scriptural proof |
|     and was seen |   2b) Physical proof |

In summoning the evidence for his propositions, Paul is arguing his case like any good lawyer (the possible oxymoron noted!). A brief explanation of each of the statements follows.

*Christ died for our sins.* The concept of "Christ" may not have been entirely understood by the Corinthian readers, but the meaning of *anointed* and His work of dying for sins certainly points to a special divine messenger. That He died for our sins implies that we are sinners in need of forgiveness. The word *for* conveys the idea of "on account of," that is, to deal with our sins.

*According to the Scriptures.* The Old Testament Scriptures pictured or predicted the suffering of God's Messiah.[2]

*And was buried.* This statement functions as Jesus' death certificate. It reminds the reader of the many eyewitnesses to His death, the best evidence which could be summoned. Only *dead* men are buried. Christ's death was witnessed by multitudes, including the soldier sent to break His legs. The grave and body were also attended by Joseph of Arimathea, Nicodemus, and the women.

*He arose.* The second proposition attests to Christ's resurrection from the dead, which implies that God accepted the sacrifice. A dead man cannot save anyone. A Savior has to be alive. Only then can He offer and effect salvation.

*According to the Scriptures.* It is harder to find the resurrection of Christ in the Old Testament. It is there, however, not only explicitly (Pss. 16:8–11; 110:1), but also implicitly. When the suffering and death of the Messiah is discussed, this is sometimes followed by a declaration of His reign (Isaiah 53). The implication is clearly that He rose from the dead.

*And was seen.* Paul lists those who were eyewitnesses. This includes the apostles, men of repute; a multitude of five hundred; and himself (1 Cor. 15:5–8).

## A CLEAR CONDITION

Just when I had talked myself into the benefit of becoming involved with my community's ministerial alliance, they decided to launch a community-wide evangelistic survey. A smorgasbord subcommittee of pastors designed the evangelistic tract that would be handed out door to door. To be thorough, I guess, the tract covered all the bases. It spoke of believing in Jesus as Savior (Amen!), but went on to tell the poor chap at the door, who was probably dying to get back to his television ASAP, that he must *confess his sins, call on the name of the Lord, open the door of his heart, receive Jesus as Savior and Lord, and let Him take control of the throne of his life.* The problem is not that all of this language is unbiblical, which most of it is, but it is so *confusing.* Since the alliance would not let our church use different literature, I had to drop out of my first foray into cooperative evangelism. The reverends were miffed.

As we have shown in this book, the grace of the gospel means that the only condition for salvation is "faith alone in Christ alone." But this is where much gospel-telling takes a space-walk. Let's review some language commonly used to explain the condition of salvation.

*Ask Jesus into your heart.* It's true that the heart is universally understood as the very essence of our being and person. But in this phrase, the issue of trust in Jesus as one who died in our place is hardly communicated. And wouldn't this be confusing to a child who thinks concretely instead of abstractly? James Dobson related this story on a radio broadcast: As a mother drove her young daughter in the car, Mom was explaining what it meant to have Jesus in her heart. The little girl leaned over and put her ear to her mother's chest. "I'm listening to Jesus in your heart," said the daughter. "What did you hear?" asked the Mom. The little girl replied, "Sounds to me like He's making coffee!"

*Give your heart (or life) to God.* A Halloween gospel tract designed for children to leave at homes when trick-or-treating ends with, "Well, thanks again for the treat, but the best treat for me would be for you to give your heart to Jesus." Oh, how appropriate for Halloween! A child might imagine this as a gruesome display for the local haunted house. Again, picture the scene it conveys to a naive child. An evangelist tells how one child, when asked to give his heart to God, broke into sobs saying, "If I give my heart to God, how am I going to live?" The issue in salvation is not what we give to Him anyway, but *what He gives to us.* Eternal life is Christ's life in us (1 John 5:11).

*Invite Christ into your life.* This is certainly a courteous approach. But we must remember that it is the Lord who does the inviting. Another form of this is the admonition to "open the door of your heart," based on Revelation 3:20. I used to use this verse a lot, but I now see that it was written to the Laodicean church as a whole and was more of an invitation for fellowship than salvation. Again, after you get a child to stop wondering where the knob on the door of his heart is, you've really told him nothing about what it means to believe in Christ. Adults are not helped either.

*Receive Christ as your Savior.* This one I hesitate to criticize, and even find myself using it sometimes, though I try to avoid it. There *is* some biblical support for the idea of receiving Christ: John 1:11–12 and Colossians 2:6. Both uses, however, are in the past tense, pointing to the result of faith. Receiving Christ, though, is what happens when we believe—or have faith—and He comes to live in us. Further, the context of both passages refers to faith as the condition for salvation. *Accept Christ* is similar, but not used for faith in Christ in the New Testament.

*Make Christ Lord and Savior.* Spare the effort. No person can do this. The Bible says *God the Father* "has made this Jesus . . . both Lord and Christ" (Acts 2:36). Of course Jesus is Lord! But He is Lord whether we accept Him as such or not.

*Make Christ Lord of your life.* This language misleads unbelievers when used as a condition for salvation. Lordship decisions are decisions for *Christian* obedience made by *believers* in the light of transforming grace (Titus 2:11–12), not something *done to merit* that grace (Titus 3:4–7). Sometimes we hear "If He is not Lord of all, He is not Lord at all." Would somebody please tell me what this saying means?

*Put Jesus on the throne of your life.* In other words, give Him control of all areas of your life. Has anyone accomplished this? It is a commendable admonition for a believer, but again is misleading to use with an unbeliever as a condition for salvation. It is better to deal with this issue after a person understands the issue of faith in Christ for salvation. I know, however, that some people believe in Christ as Savior and surrender to Him as Lord, simultaneously. They inherently understand that if Christ saves us, He also deserves to rule us, and both decisions appear as one. Still, the issues are distinct.

*Confess your sins.* To a priest? How many sins? What about ones that are overlooked, forgotten, unintentional, or by omission? This is confusing. We must all acknowledge, of course, that we are sinners before God, and we confess this to Him when we agree with Him that we are, indeed, sinners. The word translated "confess" literally means "to speak the same thing" or "to agree with." We are saved *from something*, and that is our sin. But the above statement implies our problem is specific individual acts rather than our sinful position or nature. God wants to cure the cause not the symptoms.

*Repent of your sins.* Sometimes less sensitively stated as "Turn or burn!" If by this it is meant that we must turn from every individual sin in our lives, then salvation and assurance would be impossible. Repentance in the New Testament speaks of an inner change of attitude and heart, not an outer change in conduct. Changed conduct is the expected result of true repentance, but we should not confuse the root with the fruit. As we come to faith we may change our minds about a number of things—our sinful status before God, for example, or our need for salvation, or our opinion of who Christ is.

*Pray this prayer.* We should not give someone the impression that they can be saved by a ritual such as prayer. It is better to tell them that they must believe in Christ, and they can tell Him *through* prayer that they want the gift of eternal life or that they are thankful for what He has done.

Not all of the above conditions are totally void of all truth. The point is that they are often misleading or confusing. Why not be as biblical as possible in our communication of the condition for salvation? In the gospel of John the verb *believe* is used ninety-eight times as the condition for salvation. We should take the hint, especially when the Holy Spirit had John tip us off that he wrote his book in order to bring people to faith in Christ (John 20:31). We don't find any of the above language there, except as noted above, the mention of receiving Christ found in John 1 and Colossians 2.

## A CLEAR INVITATION

A minister acquaintance told me an *almost* humorous story of his conversion. When he was a totally pagan, longhaired bartender and bouncer, he attended a church meeting and went forward at the evangelist's invitation. When he got to the front, the host pastor met him and asked, "Do you come to make a profession of faith in Christ?" Bill looked confused. The pastor asked several times. Bill finally said, "Look, I don't know what you're talking about. I just want Jesus." He told me if it had not been for the evangelist's clarity in the sermon, he would not have found Christ up front with the pastor. As one of my seminary professors was fond of saying, "A mist in the pulpit is a fog in the pew."

A clear telling of the gospel can easily become unclear when the invitation is given. Whether it is an invitation in a one-on-one encounter or a public invitation by a preacher, there are certain things that will keep it clear. Here are some of the common invitations and comments on each.

*Come forward.* The invitation to come down the church aisle is used by many preachers, though criticized by others—sometimes rightly so. It *has* only been around since the 1800s. Some people will quickly respond to such a public expression, and others would rather go through an IRS audit before they'd stand up in front of a crowd. Walking the aisle is not harmful if the person clearly understands the issue. We probably all know someone who came to faith in this way. But people should never be led to believe that they *must* walk an aisle in order to be saved. They could be encouraged to walk an aisle if they want to talk to someone about their salvation or if they want to make a public statement that they have trusted in Jesus Christ as Savior during the meeting.

*Bow your heads and close your eyes.* (Not *Close your heads and bow your eyes,* as one hapless preacher stated it!) Why must people always get saved with their eyes closed? In a séance, opening the eyes might break the spell, but in a gospel confrontation faith can appear with eyes wide open. Funny, but Jesus was always *opening* peoples' eyes! On the serious side, closed eyes and bowed heads can create a safe, confidential, and prayerful environment for those who may want to respond publicly.

*Raise your hand.* Again, we must avoid implying that a physical act is necessary. Raising a hand, however, is less threatening to a person than walking an aisle. It may give the preacher more opportunity to identify those who are interested in salvation. I, in fact, sometimes ask people to raise their hands in a group invitation, because I want to follow up with them. I will often tell them something like this:

> You don't have to bow your head or raise your hand
> to be saved. You can believe in Jesus Christ with your
> eyes wide open while you're looking at me. I would
> just like to know that you have placed your faith in

Christ as your Savior or that you want to know more about that. The only way I can know who you are, so I can speak with you later in private, is if you raise your hand. I really would like to talk to you about it.

*Sign a card.* This is also non-threatening to many people. Asking people to sign a card is often unwise unless *all* the people present at the meeting fill out cards, which makes people feel less conspicuous. A card could include these categories to check:

- I have trusted in Jesus Christ as my Savior today.
- I want more information about knowing Jesus Christ as Savior.
- I want to know for certain that I have eternal life.
- I want to speak to someone about my salvation.

*Pray a prayer.* An invitation involving prayer *can* be handled correctly. The gospel-teller must be careful to make the issue faith. When inviting people to Christ, I explain how Christ saves us through faith, I make sure they understand the issues, then I ask, "Do you believe this?" If they say "Yes," I say, "Then why don't you thank Him right now in prayer for dying for you and for giving you eternal life?"

It may not be possible to validate a public invitation from the Scriptures. But then we could not validate using gospel tracts and evangelism training classes either. Sharing the Good News implies an invitation to believe, and giving a clear invitation may help many to actually do it. The main point in relation to the invitation is this: we don't want a person to get faith mixed up with works. If we have told someone that salvation is a free gift, then we must be consistent and not demand any action as a condition. When someone decides to respond to any kind of invitation, it seems logical, in fact, that they are already trusting in Christ and just desire to express it somehow.

Clear communication is an art. When it comes to sharing the gospel, it is an art worth refining. We must work to tell the gospel as clearly as possible. Not always will we succeed. But isn't it a wonderful fact of life that God can still use us in spite of the misplaced approaches and methods that we use? We know, however, that He can accomplish more through us according to how clear and biblical our message and our methods are. And that means that we are clear in our gospel content, in our statement of the condition for salvation, and in our invitation to believe. Given all that is at stake, we want to share the Good News as clearly as possible in a way that is pleasing to God, not just convenient to men.

We give the last word to the Bible. "But as we have been approved by God to be entrusted with the gospel, even so we speak, not as pleasing men, but God who tests our hearts" (1 Thess. 2:4).